WARCRAFT
REIGN OF CHAOS
D0180579
FAVORED
OF THE
THE KALDO
BUILT
GIANT
DEEP INTO THE
MOUNTAINS AND FORESTS OF

Blizzard Entertainment. P.O. Box 18979, Irvine, CA 92623

(800) 953-SNOW	Direct Sales
(949) 955-0283	International Direct Sales
(949) 737-SNOW	Technical Support Fax
(949) 955-1382	Technical Support
http://www.blizzard.com	World Wide Web
support@blizzard.com	Online Technical Support
macsupport@blizzard.com	Macintosh Online Technical Support

CONTENTS

Getting Started

PC System Requirements

COMPUTER: 400 MHz processor or better.

OPERATING SYSTEMS: Windows 98, Windows ME, Windows 2000, or Windows XP.

MEMORY: Warcraft III requires 128 MB of RAM.

CONTROLS: A keyboard and mouse are required. Joysticks, game pads, graphics tablets, and input devices other than a mouse and keyboard are not supported.

DRIVES: A hard drive with at least 700 MB of free space, and a 4x speed CD-ROM drive are required for installation and play.

VIDEO: 8 MB 3D video card with DirectX 8.1 support (TNT, i810,Voodoo3, Rage 128 equivalent or better)**Please visit our website for a comprehensive list of supported 3D video cards at **http://www.blizzard.com/support/**

SOUND: A DirectX compatible 16-bit sound card is required.

MULTIPLAYER CONNECTIVITY: Access to Blizzard Entertainment's online gaming service, Battle.net, requires a low-latency, active Internet connection, rated at 28.8 Kbps or faster. Multi-player games played over a LAN require an active connection to a TCP/IP network.

Installation

Place the Warcraft III disc into your CD-ROM drive. If your computer is AutoPlay capable, the Warcraft III Installer menu will automatically appear on the screen. Select "Install Warcraft III" from the list to start the installation process. Follow the on-screen instructions. After the game is successfully installed, a Warcraft III shortcut is added to your Start menu.

If your system is not AutoPlay capable, open the My Computer icon on your Desktop, then select the drive letter that represents your CD-ROM drive. Double-click the install.exe or Setup icon, and continue as set forth in the paragraph above.

Installation of DirectX

Make sure that the Warcraft III disc is in your CD-ROM drive. When you begin the installation process, Warcraft III automatically detects whether or not your version of DirectX needs to be updated. Should you need to update your version of DirectX, you will be prompted to do so. As Warcraft III cannot be played without DirectX, we recommend installing DirectX immediately should you be directed. The latest version of DirectX can be found on Microsoft's website at **http://www.microsoft.com/directx/**

If you experience any problems installing Warcraft III, please see our Troubleshooting section before contacting technical support.

Mac® System Requirements

COMPUTER: Warcraft III requires a 400 MHz G3 processor or better.

OPERATING SYSTEM: Warcraft III requires Mac OS® 9.0 or higher, or Mac OS X® 10.1.3 or higher.

MEMORY: Warcraft III requires 128 MB of RAM. Virtual Memory should be enabled on computers running pre-Mac OS X versions of the Mac OS®.

CONTROLS: A keyboard and mouse are required. Joysticks, game pads, graphics tablets, and input devices other than a mouse and keyboard are not supported.

DRIVES: A hard drive with at least 700 MB of free space, and a 4x speed CD-ROM drive are required for installation and play.

Video: A video card consisting of an ATI Technologies or nVidia chipset with at least 16 MB of memory is required.

SOUND: Warcraft III will work with the built-in sound features of the Mac OS®.

MULTIPLAYER CONNECTIVITY: Access to Blizzard Entertainment's online gaming service, Battle.net, requires a low-latency, active Internet connection rated at 28.8 Kbps or faster. Multi-player games played over a LAN require an active connection to a TCP/IP network.

Installation

Place the Warcraft III disc into your CD-ROM drive. Double-click on the Warcraft III CD icon, and then double-click on the Warcraft III Installer application to copy the required game files to your hard drive. The installer will present an abbreviated readme document. Please read this, as it contains additional up-to-date information about Warcraft III.

Starting the Game

First, confirm that you have installed Warcraft III onto your hard drive. Next, make sure that the Warcraft III disc is in your CD-ROM drive. Find the Warcraft III icon on your hard drive, and double-click on it. The Main Menu screen will be displayed, and from this screen, you can start a single-player campaign game, initiate a multi-player game, or access the game options menus.

Troubleshooting [PC]

GENERAL LOCKUPS/VIDEO PROBLEMS

If your computer hard locks without an error message, reboots during game play, will not start, or has distorted graphics of any sort, please make sure that you have the latest video card drivers for your 3D accelerator. Contact your hardware manufacturer to find the latest drivers available, or check our support website for links to the most common hardware vendors at **http://www.blizzard.com/support/**

SOUND ISSUES

If you are experiencing sound distortions, periodic loss of sound, loud squelches, whistles, or pops, confirm that you have the latest version of DirectX installed on your system. Also, verify that your sound drivers are compatible with the newest version of DirectX. Contact your hardware manufacturer to find the latest drivers available, or check our support website for links to the most common hardware vendors at **http://www.blizzard.com/support/**

Try each 'Sound Provider' setting in the game's sound options menu. You should also try toggling positional audio and environmental effects on and off in the sound options menu.

Troubleshooting [Mac®]

If you encounter an install or game play problem on a computer running a pre-Mac OS X version of the Mac OS®, open the Extension Manager control panel, choose the Mac OS Base set from the Selected Set choice bar, and restart the computer. Then try to install or play Warcraft III again.

SINGLE BUTTON MICE

With a single-button mouse, hold down the **Command** (⌘) key on the keyboard while you click the mouse button to simulate a right-click in the game.

On computers running a pre-Mac OS X version of the Mac OS® there are options available to provide multi-button mouse support, and you can access them via the game's Main Menu. From the Main Menu screen, click on the Options button, and then click on the Gameplay Options button. Then enable the checkbox labeled Multi-Button Mouse Support.

Mac OS X automatically supports multi-button mice.

Game Performance

If you encounter slow or choppy game play, there are several game options that can be adjusted to improve performance. These options are accessible via the Options button in the Main Menu screen. Selecting a lower resolution in the video options screen, turning off music, and turning off positional audio in the sound options screen, will have the greatest effect.

Additional troubleshooting material is available in the readme located on the Warcraft III disc.

Technical Support Contacts

Web Support

The Blizzard Entertainment Technical Support website has solutions to the most common game questions and problems. This free service is available 24 hours a day, 7 days a week. You can find our Technical Support website at **http://www.blizzard.com/support/**

For updated information about protecting your computer and Battle.net account, along with answers to commonly asked questions, go to **http://www.blizzard.com/support/information/warning.shtml**

Email Support

You can email our Technical Support department any time. Under normal circumstances, you will receive an automated reply within 15 minutes detailing solutions to the most common problems. Typically, within 24 to 72 hours, you will receive a second email containing a more detailed solution to your particular problem or question.

For PC support, email **support@blizzard.com**
For Macintosh support, email **macsupport@blizzard.com**

Online Chat Support

Using your Blizzard Entertainment game and your Internet connection, you can chat with a live technician through our Battle.net service. This free Technical Support service is offered Monday through Friday from 10 A.M. to 12 P.M. and from 2 P.M. to 6 P.M., Pacific Standard Time (except on U.S. holidays), and is only available on the US West gateway.

Automated Phone Support

Our automated phone support is offered 24 hours a day, 7 days a week and has an 80% success rate addressing the most common questions and concerns. To use this automated phone support, please call (949) 955-1382 and when instructed, select option 2. Automated support carries no additional charge beyond any normal long-distance charges assessed by your phone company for calls outside of your local area.

Live Phone Support

We offer live phone support Monday through Friday from 9 A.M. to 6 P.M., Pacific Standard Time (except on U.S. holidays). Contact our Technical Support staff by calling us at (949) 955-1382. Live phone support carries no additional charges beyond any normal long-distance charges assessed by your phone company for calls outside of your local area. Please be sure to consult our troubleshooting section before calling Technical Support, and be near your computer if possible when calling. NO GAME-PLAYING HINTS WILL BE GIVEN THROUGH THIS NUMBER.

Additional Support Services

You can also contact Blizzard Technical Support via fax at (949) 737-2000 or by mail at

Technical Support
Blizzard Entertainment
P.O. Box 18979
Irvine, CA
92623

Game Hints

If you are seeking a game tips, hints, or additional game information for Warcraft III, please visit **http://www.battle.net/war3**

The Game

Game Menus

When you start playing Warcraft III, the Main Menu is the first game screen that you see. From here you can start a **S**ingle-player game, enter **B**attle.net, select your Battle.net Gateway, launch a **L**ocal Area Network game, adjust game **O**ptions, view the **C**redits, or **Q**uit Warcraft III by left-clicking on the appropriate button. Note that one letter on each command button is distinct from the other letters. This letter corresponds to a hotkey, which, when pressed on your keyboard, achieves the same result as clicking on the button itself. This convention is used throughout this manual, the game menus, and in the game itself.

SINGLE-PLAYER MENU: To play the Warcraft III single-player campaigns, to play games against computer opponents, or to learn how to play, left-click this menu button.

BATTLE.NET MENU: To play games on Blizzard's Battle.net gaming service, click on the **B**attle.net button. For more information refer to the Battle.net section of the manual.

BATTLE.NET GATEWAY: The small magnifying glass button will take you to the Gateway selection menu. For details regarding Gateways go to the Battle.net section of this manual.

LOCAL AREA NETWORK MENU: To play games against opponents over your Local Area Network, select this button.

OPTIONS MENU: This menu is used to change the game's video, sound and gameplay options. See the options section later in the manual for details.

CREDITS: Many talented people worked to bring you Warcraft III. Click this button to see who they are.

QUIT: Left-clicking this button will close the Warcraft III program. You can also quickly quit the game at any time by pressing **Alt+F4.**

The Single-Player Game

Your Single-Player Profile

When you first begin a single-player game, you will be prompted to create a profile. All of your saved single-player games and replays will then be stored under a folder of the same name as your profile. Additional player profiles can be created and managed through this menu.

Starting a Campaign

To start a single-player campaign from the single-player menu, left-click the **C**ampaign button. There are five campaigns that comprise the overall Warcraft III story. The first campaign is a tutorial, where you learn the basics of control and gameplay, as taught to you by the young Orc warchief, Thrall. In each of the following campaigns, you will play one of the four playable races: the Human Alliance, Undead Scourge, Orc Horde, and Night Elf Sentinels. You cannot play campaigns out of order, but you can return to previous missions in the campaigns to replay them.

SEAMLESS QUESTS

Each campaign mission is comprised of a series of quests, but the transition between these scenarios is a seamless one. There are no "mission briefing" screens to take you out of the action. Instead, your quests in Warcraft III are given to you either by major characters or through short movies that play within the game itself. In this way, the pace and mood of each campaign are maintained without any interruption.

QUEST SCREEN

If, at any time during a campaign mission, you wish to view your quests, you can click on the Quests button at the top of the screen to see a list of your primary and optional quests. Successfully resolving primary quests is necessary to complete the scenario. If you fail in a primary quest, the scenario will end in defeat.

Optional quests are not initially revealed to you, and only become available after encountering certain areas or characters. These quests are not necessary in order to achieve victory in your current scenario, but completing them will often make accomplishing your primary quests easier to achieve or give you a special reward.

Loading a Saved Game

You can save your game at any time during a campaign mission. You can also save your progress while playing a custom game. To resume your campaign or custom game, click on the **L**oad Saved Game button from the single-player menu. Your saved games are organized into different directories depending on whether they are campaign games or custom games.

Viewing a Replay

Every time you complete a mission, you have the opportunity to save a replay of it so you can review your game. To view a replay, simply click the View **R**eplay button. When you click on the View **R**eplay button, you will be taken to a replay menu that lists all the available replays, organized into folders according to the type of games played. Once you select a replay file, you can play it and watch your game in its entirety at different speeds and even from another player's perspective.

Replays are an excellent way to watch how you play and learn from your mistakes or accomplishments. You can only view replays with Warcraft III. However, you can trade replays with other Warcraft III owners and view their replays as well.

Playing a Custom Game

From the single-player menu you can also play custom games, which are games against one or more computer opponents. To play a custom game, left-click the Custom **G**ame option from this screen. You can then choose from a variety of team configurations, maps, and game settings before you embark on a game.

CHOOSING A MAP

After entering the custom game menu, you will see a list of folders at the top left of your screen. All of the available maps included with Warcraft III are divided among the folders here. Maps specially designed for custom games, maps commonly used in multi-player games, and player-created maps are available among these folders. You must first click on the appropriate map folder, then click on the specific map you desire.

CHOOSING TEAM CONFIGURATIONS

Once you have selected a map, configure your team in the Pre-game Chat screen. Each player chooses a race, team, and color, while the game creator can close available slots or assign them as computer players. Setting same team affiliation will ally those players at game start.

Computer opponents can be set to fight against you and each other, or you can choose to play a game where all computer opponents only attack you. You can also decide to play a Team Game pitting you and a computer ally against multiple computer opponents, or choose from any number of other available combinations by carefully setting the team affiliations.

ADVANCED OPTIONS

For additional advanced options click on the Advanced **O**ptions button from the Custom Game Map screen. From this menu, you can alter parameters such as whether to play with random races and random Heroes, how much of the map is initially visible, the number of computer opponents you will face, and other options.

Battle.net®

REQUIRES: A 32-bit TCP/IP connection to the Internet. This can either be a direct connection or a dial-up connection.

Battle.net is Blizzard Entertainment's free Internet gaming service. It allows players from around the world to battle against each other. Battle.net supports a worldwide ranking system, enabling you to test your Warcraft III skills against comparable opponents. Connecting to Battle.net is easy. Simply connect to the Internet or configure your computer to automatically connect, then select Battle.net from the Main Menu. Once on Battle.net, you can chat with other players, create and join games. New Battle.net features introduced in Warcraft III include anonymous matchmaking, and a Friends list. These new features are described elsewhere in this section.

GATEWAY SELECTION

Gateways act as portals through which players get onto Battle.net. Gateways are named to indicate where your closest Gateway server is located, directing you to the best connection and play experience. While it is best to choose the Gateway closest to your geographic location, you are not restricted to any particular Gateway.

You can change your Gateway of entry before connecting to Battle.net. The small Magnifying Glass button next to the Battle.net button is the Gateway selection button. A default Gateway is already chosen for you. If you experience connection problems while using your current Gateway, simply log out and choose a new Gateway from the pull-down menu.

Waiting Room

When you first connect to Battle.net, you are taken to a Warcraft III "waiting room." A variety of options are available to you using the buttons at the top of this window. You can choose to Play **G**ame, play a **T**eam game, play a **C**ustom game, manage your **F**riends list, view Ladder **I**nfo, or enter a chat Channe**l**. For more information about each of these options, simply move your cursor and pause over the appropriate button to call up a tooltip that explains the button in more detail.

Anonymous Matchmaking

Anonymous matchmaking is a new feature on Battle.net that matches Warcraft III players of similar skill level together for a game. To play a game with anonymous allies and opponents select the Play Game button. You can then specify what game type you want to play, how many players, and what maps you are willing to play on. When you are satisfied with your choices and join a

game, Battle.net looks for other players in your Gateway of comparable skill who wish to play the same game type and maps as you. Battle.net determines your skill level by looking at various criteria including your rating on Battle.net, the number of games you have played, and your win-loss record.

MAP PREFERENCES FOR ANONYMOUS MATCHMAKING GAMES

Both the Play Game and Arranged Team options allow you to indicate what maps you prefer to play on by clicking on the thumbs up or thumbs down buttons next to the name of the maps that are available for play. The map will be automatically and randomly chosen from amongst the maps that received the most thumbs up votes. If you are in a big game, you may wind up playing on a map that you don't prefer.

Arranged Team Games

If you wish to play games against anonymous opponents but wish to play with teammates of your choosing, you can opt to play arranged team games. In these games, you choose your allies before launching a game. To play an arranged team game, click the Arranged Team button from the waiting room or chat room. Once you and all of your allies have entered the team game screen, you can launch a game, and Battle.net will look for similar teams to match you against. As with anonymous matchmaking games, you do not know who your opponents are beforehand, and you do not necessarily know on what map you will play.

Ladder Information

The ladder is an official ranking of Warcraft III players. The results of all games played using the Play Game and Arranged Team options are recorded and reflected in the players' profiles. The icon by your name in chat rooms will change as your ladder status changes. Players move up or down on the ladder according to their success or failure in anonymous matchmaking games. Ladder statistics are updated daily. For more information go to **http://www.battle.net/war3**

Custom Game

If you wish to play a game without anonymous opponents and with a map of your choice, you can choose to play a custom game. A custom game allows you to play with people you know as well as play on a specific map. Once you select a custom game, you will be taken to the custom game screen. At the left of your screen you will see a list of available games. Clicking on a game will reveal information about the map and the game's host in the map window on the upper right-hand side of the screen.

Create and Join Game

When you have chosen a game to play, left-click on its name in the Available Games List, then click **J**oin Game to enter it. If you wish to create your own game, click **C**reate Game from this screen, give your game a name, choose a map, decide on teams for all players and computer players, then specify whether the game will be a public or private game. If you elect to create a private game, you must then create a password that players must enter before they can join your game.

Friends List

As you play Warcraft III on Battle.net, you may find particular players with whom you enjoy playing and chatting. You can choose to add these players to your Friends list. This allows you to keep track of your friends by letting you know when they log onto Battle.net as well as alerting you when they enter Chat Channels or create games. For more information on how to manage your Friends list, direct your web browser to **http://www.battle.net/chat/friends.shtml** .

Channel

From the waiting room, you can click on the **E**nter Chat button to go directly to a default chat channel. You may also click on the Channe**l** button to open the channel menu, where you can select your desired channel from a list of available channels or, if you know of a private channel, type in a specific channel name. Once you enter a channel, you can begin chatting with the other players who are also logged onto Battle.net and in the same channel as you. The same options that exist in a waiting room are also available in a Chat Channel.

Local Area Network Menu

Local Area Network

To play a multi-player game over a local area network, left-click the Local Area Network button in the multi-player menu.

REQUIRES: Two or more computers connected to an active 32 bit TCP/IP compatible network.

Once you elect to play a Local Area Network (LAN) game, you will be prompted to create a player name for yourself. You will be known by this name when chatting with other players in your local area network and during the games themselves. In a LAN game you can create and join games using the same custom game options available on Battle.net.

Options Menu

The Options screen is where you can modify how Warcraft III looks, sounds, and plays to suit your hardware and your own preferences. To access the options menu, click the **O**ptions button on the Main Menu. The options may also be accessed during a game by hitting **F10** and then left-clicking on the **O**ptions button in the menu. The options available to the player are divided into three categories: Gameplay, Video, and Audio. Note that some options are only modifiable from the Main Menu, and not while in a game. Many video and audio options have multiple settings. Players with less powerful systems should choose lower settings to increase game performance. To further enhance performance certain settings, such as music or ambient sounds, can be disabled altogether.

Gameplay Options

GAME SPEED (Only modifiable while playing a single-player game)

This slider bar controls the pace of the game.

MOUSE SCROLL

This slider bar controls how fast the game screen pans when the mouse cursor is moved to the edge of the screen.

DISABLE MOUSE SCROLL

Checking this box disables use of the mouse to scroll around the map; instead, you must use the arrow keys on your keyboard.

KEYBOARD SCROLL

This slider bar controls how fast the game screen pans when the arrow keys are used to scroll the map.

ENHANCED TOOLTIPS

If this box is checked, the Enhanced Tooltips will be displayed to the player. Enhanced Tooltips provide additional information about an icon when you move and hold your cursor over it.

Video Options

GAMMA

This slider bar controls the gamma setting for the game screen. Users who find the game screen too dark should try increasing the gamma setting to the right, closer to Bright.

RESOLUTION (Only modifiable from the Main Menu options screen)
This setting has the greatest impact on overall graphic performance. This option adjusts the resolution and color depth of the game display. The lower your resolution, the faster the game will perform as fill rate decreases. If you experience poor performance, we recommend reducing your resolution and color depth until performance becomes acceptable.

MODEL DETAIL (Only modifiable from the Main Menu options screen)
Choose between Low, Medium, and High model detail settings. Low detail models use fewer polygons, while High detail models use more polygons to create a smoother look to the unit.

ANIMATION QUALITY (Only modifiable from the Main Menu options screen)
This option adjusts animation blending and animation smoothness. There are three quality settings: LOW, MEDIUM, and HIGH. Setting this option to LOW increases performance and reduces memory use. If you are running on a system with 128 MB of system memory, we recommend setting this option to LOW.

TEXTURE QUALITY (Only modifiable from the Main Menu options screen)
Choose between texture resolutions of Low, Medium, and High quality. Lower quality textures will appear less sharp in the game, while High quality textures have the most detail.

PARTICLES
This option adjusts the number of particles drawn per emitter. Altering these settings can change the appearance of certain spell effects, footprints, weather, waves, etc. There are three quality settings: LOW, MEDIUM, and HIGH. LOW draws approximately one third of the total particles. MEDIUM draws approximately two thirds of the total particles. HIGH draws 100% of the total particles. We recommend reducing your particle setting if you are experiencing slow downs during large battles.

LIGHTS
This option controls the number of lights rendered per object. There are three quality settings: LOW, MEDIUM, and HIGH. LOW uses one light. MEDIUM uses four lights. HIGH uses eight lights. If you have an older graphics card with 16 MBs or less memory, we recommend setting this option to LOW.

Sound Options

SOUND EFFECTS VOLUME
Use this slider bar to adjust the volume of the game's sound effects. You may also turn the sound effects completely off by leaving the checkbox to the left of the slider bar unchecked. To toggle sound on or off at any point in the game, press the **Ctrl+S** hotkey.

MUSIC VOLUME
Use this slider bar to adjust the game's music volume. You may also turn the music completely off by leaving the checkbox to the left of the slider bar unchecked. Turning off the music can provide a slight increase in performance on some systems. To toggle music on or off at any point in the game, press the **Ctrl+M** hotkey.

AMBIENT SOUNDS

Check this box to enable the ambient environmental sounds present in the game. Doing so provides a slight decrease in performance on some systems.

MOVEMENT SOUNDS

Check this box to enable the sounds units produce when moving.

SUBTITLES

Check this box to enable dialog subtitles.

UNIT SOUNDS

Check this box to enable the acknowledgement sounds played when a unit is selected.

SOUND PROVIDER (Only modifiable from the Main Menu options screen)

This dropdown menu shows which sound providers are available for use on your system. Different sound providers could provide different levels of performance on your system. You should consult your sound card's documentation to see which option is best suited for your system before changing this setting.

ENVIRONMENTAL EFFECTS

Enable the use of Environmental Effects such as reverb and echo by checking this checkbox. Disabling Environmental Effects can cause an increase in performance on some systems.

POSITIONAL AUDIO

Enable the use of 3D Positional Audio in the game by checking this checkbox. Disabling Positional Audio can cause an increase in performance on some systems.

Controls

Using the Keyboard and Mouse

You will spend most of your time controlling your units and buildings with the mouse in Warcraft III. The mouse is your primary means of control, although advanced players use many keyboard shortcuts to complement their mouse control.

LEFT-CLICKING

To select a unit or building, left-click on the object. To select a group of units, you must hold down the left mouse button and drag a box around the units that you wish to select. To deselect a unit, **Shift**+ left-click the unit. You also use the left mouse button to select building options, such as training a new unit or researching a new ability, and to select menu options.

RIGHT-CLICKING (Auto-commands)

To issue auto-commands to your units, you use the right mouse button. If you have a unit or group of units selected and right-click on a unit, building, or location, the game will automatically issue the most relevant command to the unit or units selected. Macintosh users can hold down the **Command (⌘)** button and click with the mouse to simulate the right-click function.

If you right-click on an enemy unit, your selected troops will automatically approach and attack the selected enemy.

If you right-click on a location, your units will automatically move to that area.

If you have a building selected and right-click on a location, any new units trained from that building will automatically attack-move to and rally there when built. A banner marker called a *rally flag* is placed to mark the rally point. If you select a Town Hall building or its equivalent and right-click on a gold mine or tree, your worker units will automatically move to the resource and begin harvesting when they finish building.

If you have a worker selected and right-click on a gold mine or tree, the worker will automatically begin harvesting. You may also right-click on a damaged building or mechanical unit with a worker, and that worker will move to and begin repairing it.

REPAIRING TRANSPORTS AND BURROWS

When you right-click on a building or unit that can contain other units, such as an Orc Burrow or a Goblin Zeppelin, the worker unit will board the transport or enter the Burrow instead of repairing it. To repair these structures and units you must issue the **R**epair command instead of right-clicking on the transport.

WAYPOINTS AND MULTIPLE ORDERS

To issue multiple auto-commands, hold down the **Shift** button and right-click. Your units will move through multiple waypoints, attack multiple targets, or execute other commands in the order that they were given.

MIDDLE BUTTON

Hold down the middle mouse button while moving the mouse to scroll the main view.

IDLE WORKERS BUTTON

The number of any Idle Workers that exist in the field is displayed by an icon in the lower left-hand side of the main view screen, above the minimap. Clicking this icon will automatically select and cycle through your idle workers. Pressing the **F8** key also achieves the same function.

Moving Around the Map

To move your main view screen, you can use the arrow keys on your keyboard or move your mouse pointer to the edge of the map, whereupon the screen will move in the direction your mouse pointer is facing.

Notifications

Warcraft III provides visual and audio notifications of important game events. For example, when your units are under attack, a visual ping (see Minimap Signal section for more details) will appear on the minimap at the location of the event with an accompanying audio alert. Pressing the **Spacebar** key centers the game view where the last notification occurred. Repeatedly pressing the **Spacebar** will cycle through up to the last 8 notifications in reverse order.

Cycling Through Multiple Town Halls

If you have more than one Town Hall or its equivalent, you can quickly cycle through them by pressing the **Backspace** key. Each instance of **Backspace** will center your view on a Town Hall.

Selecting Multiple Units

In addition to dragging a box around multiple units to select more than one unit, you can select multiple units of the same type by holding the **Ctrl** key and left-clicking on one unit. You can also select multiple units of the same type by double-clicking on a unit. All other units on the screen of the same type will be selected.

Adding Units to a Group

To add units to a group, hold down the **Shift** key and left-click on the desired unit while you have your group selected. The unit will then be added to your group. To drop a unit from a group, select your group, then press **Shift** and left-click on the unit.

Bypassing Formations

When a group of units is given the Move command, they will all move in formation, occasionally pausing along the way to let slower units move into position to maintain the integrity of the formation. If you instead want the units to move to a location at best possible speed, you may hold down the **Alt** button while right-clicking on their destination.

Camera Controls

ZOOM IN AND ZOOM OUT

To zoom in your view and see the screen from a ground perspective, roll your mouse wheel forward. To pull back for a more bird's eye view, roll your mouse wheel backward. You can also press the **Page Up** and **Page Down** keys on your keyboard.

ROTATE CAMERA

Press the **Insert** and **Delete** keys on your keyboard to rotate the game camera left or right.

Keyboard Shortcuts

For a full list of keyboard shortcuts and hotkeys, see the back cover of the manual.

Game Concepts

When you first enter a game of Warcraft III, you will see your command screen. Most of the screen is dominated by your view of the world.

At the top left of the screen are tabs that allow you to access your Menu, Allies, Quests, and Chat screens.

At the top right of your screen is your resource information, showing how much gold, wood, and food you have, as well as your Upkeep level.

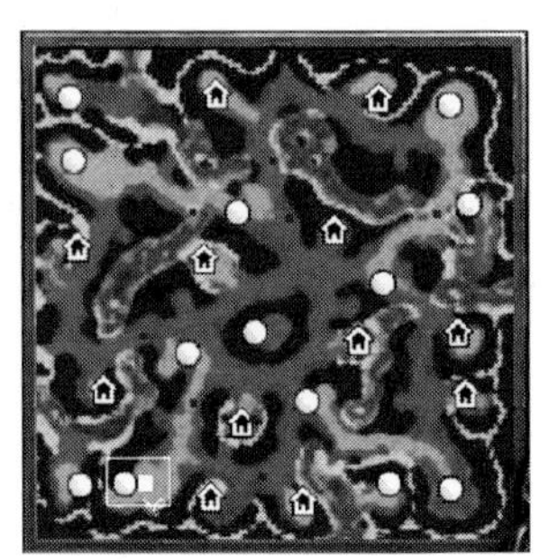

At the bottom of your screen on the left is the minimap, which shows a miniaturized view of the game map.

In the bottom center is the unit or building card showing the vital information for your selected unit or building.

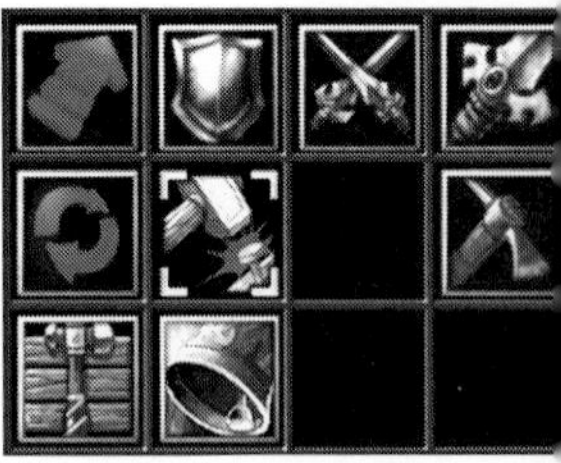

The bottom right corner of the screen shows your command card, where the various commands for your units and buildings are displayed.

Upkeep

The armies that wage war on the battlefield exact a heavy toll on the economies that support them. Even the lowliest of fighters has living expenses that must be met. Their armor must be oiled, their bows strung, and their weapons kept in clean condition. In short, these armies require Upkeep. In Warcraft III, Upkeep takes the form of a tax on your gold mining that is automatically deducted from all gold you gather. As you produce more units, the tax on your gold income increases. There are three levels of Upkeep: No Upkeep, Low Upkeep, and High Upkeep.

No Upkeep occurs when you have an army consuming 40 food or less. At this level, there is no tax on your gold mining, so your workers bring in 100 percent of their gold.

Low Upkeep arises when your army consumes between 41 and 70 food. The tax on your economy is modest, draining a small percentage of gold from everything you mine.

High Upkeep is reached when your army grows beyond 70 food. Your Upkeep needs are so great that the tax levied on your gold mining is enormous. A large percentage of gold is taken from your workers before they ever deliver it into your coffers.

Economy

Raising an army and researching new weapons of war are expensive endeavors. Soldiers demand gold, and buildings must be constructed from lumber. Creating and maintaining a thriving economy is vital to ensuring your success on the battlefield.

Each race gathers resources slightly differently, although they all must train workers with which to mine gold and harvest lumber. Some workers must gather and then return to their respective Town Hall buildings, while other races' workers use magic to move resources without needing to physically carry it back. All gold and lumber is taken to the appropriate building of each race. Human Peasants and Orc Peons can deliver lumber to special mills, while Undead Ghouls can deliver wood to their Graveyards.

Once you have gold and lumber in your reserves, you can purchase units, construct buildings, or buy upgrades. You can also give resources to your allies in team games by clicking on the Allies tab at the top of the screen.

Day/Night Cycle

At the top of your screen, you will see a small orb that will transition from a sun to a crescent moon. This timer notes the passage of time from day to night in Warcraft III. Night and Day times bring with them certain advantages and disadvantages. Orc and Human units regenerate during the day, for example, while certain

Night Elf units can become invisible at night. In addition, during nighttime, some creeps go to sleep, and the sight range of your units decreases.

Fog of War

When you begin a mission in the Warcraft III single-player campaign, a Black Mask shrouds the map. This Black Mask completely conceals the terrain features, units, and buildings present on the map. At the beginning of a game you are only able to see the immediate area around your units. Each of your units has a sight radius that reveals the nearby terrain, units, and buildings. Explore new sections of the map by moving your units into the area covered by the Black Mask.

If your units lose sight of an already explored area, that section of the map becomes covered with the Fog of War. The Fog of War conceals the presence of enemy units, but buildings and the terrain remain visible under the Fog of War. However, any changes that might occur to buildings or terrain under the Fog of War, such as building upgrades, damage, or destruction, are not shown to you.

Multi-player games of Warcraft III begin in the Fog of War. The map terrain is revealed to all players, but enemy units and buildings are still initially masked.

Enhanced Tooltips

To help you learn the game, tooltips appear whenever you move your mouse directly over an icon on the command card on the bottom right of your screen.

If you mouse over a unit icon, for example, a small box will appear above the icon showing the unit's gold, lumber, and food cost, as well as a brief description. Mousing over a building will list the building's cost and information.

If you move your mouse over a unit's special ability or spell, the tooltip will tell you the mana cost, if any, as well as the effect of the ability.

In those cases where you cannot yet build a unit or building, the enhanced tooltip box will tell you what requirements must be met before you can train or construct the unit or building.

Viewing the Minimap

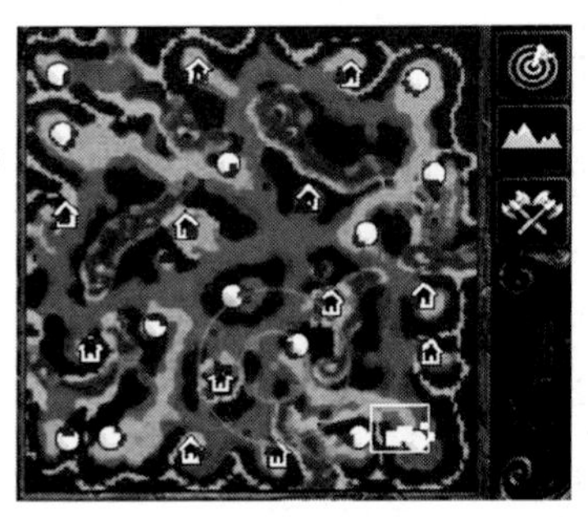

he minimap represents the entire ;ame map. The white box on the min-map indicates the current view of 'our screen. You can move the white ›ox by left-clicking on it and dragging t around, or by left-clicking on a new ocation on the minimap. Your main iew will also change as the white box n the minimap moves. You can use he minimap to quickly move your iew to different areas without having o scroll across the larger map.

MINIMAP SIGNAL

Click this button, then left-click on an area of the minimap to send a notification, or *ping*, to your allies in a multi-player game. This can be used to coordinate attacks, ask for help, or identify a waypoint to another player.

TOGGLE MINIMAP TERRAIN

Click this icon to toggle the terrain display on the minimap on and off.

TOGGLE MINIMAP ALLY COLORS

Click this icon to toggle Ally and Team colors. Ally forces will display as green points on the minimap while enemies will display as red. When you toggle the icon to show Team colors, the points on the minimap will display the Team colors that were selected before the start of the game. Regardless of how you have this set, your forces will always display as white points on the minimap.

Jnit Display

Vhen you select a unit, you will see the unit card appear at the bottom of 'our screen, displaying the following information.

ORTRAIT: A close-up view of the unit.

IIT POINTS: The unit's current and maxi-num health.

MANA: The unit's current and maximum nana, if any, which is spent on spells and pecial abilities.

NIT NAME: The name of the unit.

TATISTICS: Illustrates the unit's armor, ttack damage, attack speed, and range.

LEVEL: (Heroes only) Shows the current level of the Hero, as well as the amount of experience you need to achieve the next level.

ATTRIBUTES: (Heroes only) Displays the three attributes of Heroes – Strength, Agility, and Intelligence – that affect their health, mana, attack and armor.

INVENTORY CARD: (Heroes only) Shows the equipment currently carried by the Hero.

Command Card

This area of the screen displays the options available to you whe
you select a unit.

MOVE

Once you click on **M**ove, you must then click on a target destina
tion. The unit will move to the designated area, ignoring all ene
mies along the way (even if it is attacked).

STOP

If **S**top is clicked, the unit stops all action.

ATTACK

You must choose a target after clicking on **A**ttack. If you select a
enemy unit, your unit will move towards and attack the target
enemy until it or the target enemy dies. If you target a locatior
your unit will move to that destination, attacking any enemy uni
along the way.

ATTACK GROUND

Siege units can be ordered to attack a specific spot on the **G**roun
rather than a unit. This command can be used to attack and destro
trees.

HOLD POSITION

If you click on **H**old Position, the unit will not move to engage ene
mies in its sight range. Even if the unit is being attacked by range
fire, it will not leave its location to engage the new threat. If th
units have a ranged attack, they will attack targets of opportunit
without leaving their assigned area.

PATROL

When you click on **P**atrol, you must designate a target location o
the map. The unit will then move back and forth between the des
tination and its current position, attacking any hostile creature
that it detects. Units with active autocast spells will use ther
appropriately while on patrol.

Command Grouping

Managing an army in the thick of battle can be a burdensome endeav
or. In a particularly large skirmish, it might be hard to find your troop
and select them with the mouse. To better manage your armies, yo
can form them into command groups. You can have up to 12 units i
a group. Once you have formed a group, you can set it to a number b

pressing **Ctrl** plus a number key from **0** to **9**. If you need to recall that group again, you can press the number corresponding to that group. Pressing the number key twice in quick succession centers your view on the group.

Subgroup Controls

Warcraft III gives you an unprecedented amount of control over your grouped units. When you select multiple units together, all units of the same type are grouped together in your unit card display. Each grouping of like units in a larger group is called a subgroup. Subgroups are generally ordered from left to right according to Heroes, spellcasters, and units with abilities, with pure melee units being last.

The mini portraits of your currently selected subgroup are always highlighted and larger than the portraits of unselected subgroups. You can select the next subgroup by pressing the **Tab** button. To select the previous subgroup, press **Shift** plus **Tab**. By shifting to different subgroups within a group, you can use their special abilities or spells without ever having to deselect the group as a whole.

Follow Command

If you have a unit or a group of units selected, you can order it to follow another unit by right-clicking on a friendly or neutral unit to be followed. These units will only follow the leader, to the exclusion of attacking. This is handy to move large forces, but keep in mind that the units will only follow and will not acquire units to attack on their own.

Spells

Several units and Heroes in Warcraft III possess the ability to cast spells. Some spells improve friendly units or weaken enemy troops. Other spells do direct damage to enemies or heal allies. All spells cost a certain amount of mana to cast. Most high cost spells must be manually cast. This means you must first select the spellcaster, click on the spell icon, and then left-click on a target.

Autocast

Some spells and abilities do not need to be manually activated by the player. They are called autocast spells, and you can set them to be automatically cast by the unit when needed. To toggle a spell or ability on or off, simply right-click on the spell icon, and the borders of the spell will highlight, indicating that it will now be autocast by the computer. When the unit encounters a situation that would call for the casting of the Autocast spell, that unit will automatically cast it. For example, a Human Priest that sees a wounded friendly unit will autocast Heal

to cure the damaged unit, while an Orc Shaman will automatically cast Bloodlust on a friendly unit once that unit begins attacking an enemy target.

Passive Spells and Abilities

Some units possess abilities that do not need to be cast or even turned on. These abilities are called passive abilities, and operate as soon as the upgrade is researched. The Wyvern's Envenomed Weapon is one example. Once you research this upgrade at the Beastiary, the attacks of all your Wyverns will automatically gain the poison ability from the Envenomed Weapon. Once you research a passive ability, you will see it noted by a button in the unit's command card, even though you do not need to press it to activate the ability. It is always on.

Heroes

Each race in Warcraft III has Heroes. Heroes are special units that can be recruited at each race's Altar building. Unlike your normal units, Heroes have special qualities. They can acquire experience through battle, gain levels to improve their attributes, pick up and use magic items, and learn new spells and abilities. In Warcraft III, it is important to always have a Hero leading your armies into battle. Their powerful spells and auras of command can swing the tide of battle in your favor.

Hero Magic Resistance

As special units, Heroes enjoy a limited magic resistance against enemy spells. Negative spells cast on a Hero last a shorter duration and do less damage than if cast on a regular unit. If a Night Elf Demon Hunter and a Night Elf Archer are both stunned by an Orc Tauren Chieftain's War Stomp ability, the Demon Hunter will recover more quickly than the Archer. Likewise, if both Demon Hunter and Archer are attacked by a Human Archmage's Blizzard spell, the Demon Hunter will suffer less damage than the Archer.

First Hero is Free

Heroes normally cost gold, wood, and food. However, your first Hero in the game is always free, costing only food. When you recruit your second and third Heroes, they will cost the normal amount of gold and wood.

Experience and Level

Heroes are legendary figures that can grow in power. With each kill made by the Hero or an accompanying unit, the Hero gains experience. When enough experience has been accumulated, the

Hero gains a level. Every time a Hero advances in level, its attributes improve, its hit points and mana increase, and it gains a Hero Point that can be spent to learn special abilities or spells.

In multi-player games, all Heroes automatically come into play at first level. They begin play with one Hero Point that may be used to learn a skill or spell.

Inventory Card

Once you recruit and select a Hero, you will notice an inventory card to the right of its unit info display. As you defeat neutral monsters on the map, some will drop items on the ground, which you can retrieve and store in your inventory. Heroes are the only units that can pick up and use magic items. Each Hero can carry up to six items in its inventory card. Refer to the section on Items for more information on inventory and magic items.

Spells and Abilities

When a Hero first begins play and every time it gains a new level, it acquires a Hero Point. By clicking on the Hero Ability icon in the Hero's command card, you can choose from among four abilities to bestow on your Hero. Each Hero has one Ultimate Spell, which can only be learned once the Hero reaches the appropriate level. The other three abilities can be learned when a Hero levels up. These abilities can be spells, which must be cast to achieve an effect; passive skills, which constantly affect the Hero; or auras, which grant special bonuses to the attack, defense, or speed of any units surrounding the Hero. Most abilities have three levels of effectiveness that can be improved as additional Hero Points are spent on them. Ultimate Spells only have one level of effectiveness.

Reviving a Dead Hero

Although Heroes are larger-than-life figures, even they can die on the fields of battle. When a Hero dies, it leaves behind no corpse. As its body vanishes, the Hero's spirit returns to the ether, in order to wait recall at a sacred Altar. Each race has an Altar it can build to revive dead Heroes. There is no limit to the number of times you can revive a Hero, as long as you have enough gold to pay the revive cost. The cost of a fallen Hero depends on its level: the higher the level, the greater the cost in gold. The ritual to create a new body for the Hero takes a certain amount of time, but at its completion the Hero is revived at the Altar, along with any items the Hero carried.

Heroes in Single-Player Campaign

Heroes are handled differently in the five single-player campaigns than they are in custom games and multi-player games. In the campaigns, you do not recruit Heroes at your Altar. Instead, Heroes only come to serve you at appropriate times as dictated by each campaign's storyline. Moreover, the experience and abilities your Heroes gain will carry over from scenario to scenario in each campaign, whereas in custom and multi-player games they do not.

Wandering Monsters & Wildlife

The lands of Lordaeron are not safe. Even the indigenous creatures of the wild hold peril for the unwary wanderer. Numerous monsters called creeps camp in strategic locations on the map. Creeps, unlike the harmless critters on the map, are intelligent creatures with the means and disposition to attack all players. Creeps range in power, or level, much like Heroes. Low-level creeps are simple beasts that can be easily defeated by a few Human Footmen. However, powerful creeps are formidable adversaries capable of laying low Heroes, and some are even immune to magic. Such powerful monsters are not to be trifled with. Luckily, they are as rare as they are mighty.

All creeps are indiscriminate in their hostilities, and are ready to attack the units of any player on sight. However, these monsters will only pursue your units a limited distance. You can usually outrun them if you wish to avoid confrontation. Most creeps can be found guarding gold mines or neutral buildings.

Sleeping Creeps

The presence of creeps makes it more difficult to scout the map or execute early attacks against other players during the day. Nearly all creeps sleep at night, and during this time can be avoided with ease. It is wise to use the cover of twilight to scout, when the creeps leave wanderers undisturbed. You can recognize sleeping creeps by the animated Z over their heads and the sound of their snores. If attacked, sleeping creeps will wake to defend themselves.

Treasure

Creeps, despite their ability to attack and even kill your troops, are a boon to any player. Every creep you kill gives you gold. The amount of gold is displayed as a golden number floating above the creep's corpse immediately after it dies. Some creeps also leave

treasure chests behind. Inside the treasure chests are magic items, special objects that only Heroes can carry and that improve their effectiveness. Despite the presence of the Goblin Merchant, killing creeps is the easiest means of acquiring treasure for your Heroes. The treasure dropped is random, but the relative power of the dropped treasure is commensurate with the level of the creep. A level one creep will drop much less potent treasure than a level nine creep. The corpses left behind by dead creeps are also a treasure of sorts for the Undead commander, for these can be used by Scourge units and spells.

Experience

Creeps are not only good for treasure. They give your Heroes experience as well. Every creep killed in the vicinity of a Hero bestows a certain amount of experience points on that Hero. Thus, in multi-player games, killing creeps is an effective way of leveling up your Hero without confronting other players. Lower-level monsters, like Gnolls, give less experience than higher-level monsters, like Dragons. Fighting other players does give your Hero more experience, but early in the game, defeating creeps is the best way of quickly advancing your Heroes.

Items

Magic items are special objects that can be acquired through a variety of means. Most commonly, they are dropped at random by creeps. They can also be purchased at the Goblin Merchant's shop. Occasionally, treasure chests are also found lying unguarded on the map. Only Heroes can pick up and use items. To do so, simply right-click on the item with your Hero, who will move towards the item and place it in its inventory card.

Each Hero can carry a maximum of six items. Once an item is in your Hero's inventory, you use it by left-clicking on it. If you wish to drop an item or move it to a new space in your inventory card, you must right-click on the item. Some items require you to select a target before they can be used. Other items are automatically discharged when you left-click on them.

There are also keyboard shortcuts for quickly using your Hero's inventory items. The number keys on your keyboard's number pad correspond to the six slots on your Hero's inventory card. Pressing one of these numbers will automatically use the corresponding item. Numbers 7 and 8 represent the top row of items; numbers 4 and 5 represent the middle row of items; and numbers 1 and 2 represent the bottom row of items.

There are three types of magic items that can be found in Warcraft III: consumable, charged, and persistent.

Consumable items can be used only once, at which point they disappear from your inventory. Potions of Health are consumable items. Consumable items do not require a target. They simply act on the Hero who uses them.

Charged items can be used several times before they disappear. The number of charges the item has is displayed in the bottom right corner of the item's inventory picture. Each time you use the item, it depletes one charge until none are left, and it disappears from your inventory.

Persistent items are always on and never disappear. To cease receiving benefits from a persistent item, a Hero must drop them from its inventory. Persistent items do not require a target to be used, and give a persistent benefit to the Hero that wears them.

A Hero can carry multiple items of the same type, and the effects from multiple persistent items of the same type often stack. There are dozens of magic items that you can find throughout the game. Here are a few samples of the wondrous items you may encounter:

Scroll of Town Portal

Every Hero starts out with this item, but you can purchase more at the merchant shop or find it as random treasure. It is a one-use item that teleports the Hero and any surrounding friendly units to the selected friendly Town Hall.

Ankh of Reincarnation

This powerful item is often guarded by the fiercest of creeps. When your Hero dies, the Ankh automatically returns it to life. After its use, the Ankh disappears from your inventory.

Tome of Experience

This book is a consumable item. Left-clicking on the Tome consumes it but gives your Hero a fixed number of free experience points.

Potion of Restoration

This potion combines the effects of a Mana Potion and a Health Potion. When consumed, it fully restores your Hero's hit points and mana.

Neutral Buildings

Neutral buildings appear at strategic locations on every map in Warcraft III. They are designated on the minimap as tiny golden houses. These neutral buildings can be used by any race. Normal units cannot activate a neutral building, but any Hero that comes within close range of a neutral building can use it. When a Hero enters the vicinity of the building, an arrow usually appears over its head, indicating that the Hero can click on the neutral buildings to do business, such as hiring mercenaries or buying magic items. Some buildings have automatic benefits, and require nothing more than the presence of a Hero nearby. Here are a few neutral buildings that have been sighted in the lands of Azeroth.

Goblin Merchant

The Goblins were former allies of the Horde, but their greed has inspired them to strike out on their own. Goblin Merchants sell various magic items to visiting Heroes, including Potions of Healing, Potions of Mana, Scrolls of Town Portal, Scrolls of Healing, and Gems of True Seeing.

Fountain of Health

Unlike with other Neutral Buildings, the Fountain of Health does not need to be activated by mouse clicking. Instead, the Fountain automatically regenerates the hit points of nearby Heroes and non-mechanical units.

Goblin Laboratory

The Goblin Laboratory is a house of knowledge where you can purchase Goblin Zeppelins and Goblin Sappers. The Goblin Laboratory is also a valuable tool for scouting, as you can reveal areas of the map for a modest price here.

Goblin Zeppelin

The mechanical Goblin Zeppelin is the only transport vehicle in Warcraft III. It is necessary for those commanders who need to move their armies across otherwise impassable oceans and mountains.

Mercenary Camp

Here you will find ready fighters to join you. Many creeps that are otherwise belligerent in the wild can be bought here for a fee. Units hired will count against your overall food cap so you must have enough food to support them.

Resources

Fielding an army in Warcraft III requires a steady supply of resources. Buildings cannot be raised without wood, and soldiers will not fight without the promise of gold. The twin resources of wood and gold are the lifeblood of any army. Both can be found in ready quantities in Azeroth.

Wood

Dense forests frame the wilderness of Lordaeron. The Horde and Alliance harvest lumber with their workers, while the Undead dispatch their Ghouls to the same task. Night Elves, in contrast to the other races, do not willingly fell trees for their wood. Instead, Night Elf Wisps bond to the trees, slowly drawing on their essence to provide timber for their buildings.

Gold

Gold is a much more precious commodity than wood, accumulating in rare mines that dot the landscape. Each race mines gold differently. For Orc and Human players, only five workers can work at a gold mine at a time. Any more than that is a waste of labor, as additional Peons and Peasants will not cause you to gather gold more quickly unless, of course, your Town Hall is a long way from the gold mine. You cannot use more than five Acolytes or Wisps on one gold mine.

Food

One final resource is food. It is not harvested like wood or gold, but instead managed by building special structures that provide food. Each unit you recruit requires sustenance, although different troops consume food in varying amounts. A Peon, for example, consumes only one food, while the mighty Tauren has an appetite many times greater than that of its smaller comrade.

The Food Cap

In Warcraft III, there is a total food cap of 90 that is the same regardless of the race you play. You begin the game with a ready supply of food courtesy of your Town Hall building. Each race has a special building that can be built to increase the food cap in regular increments. The Human Alliance builds Farms, the Orcish Horde builds Burrows, the Undead Scourge builds Ziggurats, and the Night Elf Sentinels build Moon Wells. However, no matter how many such buildings you create, you cannot exceed 90 food.

Score Screen

When you finish a single-player mission or multiplayer game, you are taken to a score screen that summarizes the action of your recently completed game. You can see how well you performed, observe how much (or how little) your allies helped, and compare your score to that of other players.

Overall Score Screen

The score screen overview shows all the players involved in the game, as well as their overall score. Players are identified to the right of the screen by their name, race, and team number, if any. Their overall score is shown, as well as the score in each individual category that makes up the final total. You can further evaluate each category by clicking on the corresponding tab, which will take you to a screen that breaks down the specific category in greater detail. The highest overall score, and the highest score per category, are highlighted in yellow.

The three categories that constitute your overall score are Units, Heroes, and Resources.

UNITS SCORE SCREEN

This screen shows the number of units produced, units killed, buildings built, buildings destroyed, and the largest army.

HEROES SCORE SCREEN

This screen shows the level of each player's Heroes, the number of Heroes killed, number of items found, and the total experience gained.

RESOURCES SCORE SCREEN

This screen shows the amount of gold and lumber harvested, the amount of gold and lumber spent, the amount of gold and lumber traded, the percentage of technology researched, and the amount of gold lost to Upkeep.

Save Replay

At the score screen you also have the option of saving a replay of your completed game. The replay is saved to a replays folder in your Warcraft III directory. You can load a replay at a later date to view your entire game, from start to finish, watching not only yourself, but also all players involved. Replays are a great way to learn not only from your own performance, but from that of other players as well.

You can only view replays using Warcraft III.

World Editor

The Warcraft III World Editor is a design tool that allows players to customize many aspects of the game, as well as create entirely new maps, game types, and campaigns. The maps and campaigns created in the World Editor can be used in single-player or multiplayer games.

To launch the World Editor, open your Warcraft III folder and double-click on the World Editor icon. From your Windows Start Menu, choose Programs, Warcraft III, and click on World Editor. For the Macintosh, simply find the Warcraft III folder and double-click on the World Edit icon.

The editor is an extremely powerful tool that allows users to manipulate almost every aspect of the Warcraft III game. In order to familiarize yourself with the functionality of the editor, we strongly recommend that you load up an existing map as a point of reference.

PLEASE NOTE: Blizzard Entertainment does not directly support the editor. Our Technical Support team will be unable to answer questions about editor functionality or help resolve problems you may experience while using the editor.

For more detailed information about the Warcraft III World Editor, refer to the documentation included in the online help section of the Warcraft III disc or the World Editor itself.

Human Alliance

Human Alliance

The Human Alliance is a conglomeration of Humans, Elves, and Dwarves. They are the most versatile army in Warcraft III, with good ground and air troops, excellent siege capability, and powerful spellcasters.

Peasant Militia

The workers of the Human Alliance can be converted into Militia when the need arises. You can transform Peasants individually by clicking on the Call to Arms icon on each Peasant's command card or convert them en masse by ringing the Call to Arms bell at your Town Hall. Peasants will then rally to the Town Hall, where they don armor and wield swords to fight invaders. After a set amount of time, Militia will revert back to Peasants, or you can prematurely end their military tenure at the Town Hall with the Back to Work bell.

Cooperative Building

Humans can speed up the construction of a building by tasking extra Peasants to build and repair the structure. While the building is under construction, each additional Peasant assigned to repair the structure will ensure that the task is finished much faster. The additional Peasants will utilize extra gold and lumber to construct the building.

Sturdy Construction

Humans can improve the armor and durability of their structures at the Lumber Mill with the Improved Masonry technologies. Each upgrade provides increasing armor and hit points to the Alliance buildings.

Improved Lumber Harvesting

Two upgrades can be researched at the Lumber Mill to improve the wood gathering of the Human Alliance. Each successive upgrade increases the carrying capacity for those Peasants harvesting lumber.

Heroes

Archmage

The Archmage is a spellcasting Hero with an impressive repertoire of spells. His ranged attack can affect land and air targets. He can learn the following spells:

BLIZZARD: Damages all units in an area of effect.

SUMMON WATER ELEMENTAL: Summons an elemental to fight for the Alliance.

BRILLIANCE AURA: [Passive] Regenerates mana of Archmage and nearby friendly spellcasters at faster than normal rate.

MASS TELEPORT [Ultimate]: Teleports Archmage and your nearby troops to the location of a friendly ground unit.

Mountain King

This Hero is a melee fighter that can attack land units. He can learn the following abilities:

STORM BOLT: Hurls a hammer at one enemy unit, dealing great damage and stunning the target.

THUNDER CLAP: Slams the ground, dealing damage to all surrounding enemy ground units.

BASH: [Passive] Gives Mountain King a small chance to inflict bonus damage and stun the target when making normal melee attacks.

AVATAR: [Ultimate] Turns Mountain King into a giant, improving his armor, attack, and hit points, and making him immune to spells.

Paladin

The Paladin is a defensive fighter that can attack land units. He can learn the following powers:

HOLY LIGHT: Heals friendly unit or damages enemy undead unit.

DIVINE SHIELD: Makes Paladin temporarily invulnerable.

DEVOTION AURA: [Passive] Gives an armor bonus to all nearby friendly units.

RESURRECTION: [Ultimate] Raises a handful of slain friendly units.

Units

Peasant

Peasants construct buildings and harvest both gold and lumber for the Human Alliance. Although they possess a weak melee attack, they can be converted to more durable Militia at the Town Hall.

REPAIR: [Autocast ability] Peasants can repair all friendly buildings and mechanical units.

Militia

Militia are created from Peasants when the Call to Arms bell is rung at the Town Hall. They are unable to mine resources or raise buildings, but have a better melee attack than Peasants.

Footman

The Footman is a melee fighter that can attack other land units. It can learn the following ability:

DEFEND: Reduces the damage the Footman suffers from piercing attacks, but slows the Footman as well.

Rifleman

The Dwarven Rifleman is a ground unit with a ranged attack effective against both land and air opponents. It can benefit from the following upgrade:

LONG RIFLES: Permanently increases the range of the Rifleman.

Knight

The Knight is a fast and powerful land unit that can attack other ground targets. It can benefit from the following upgrade:

ANIMAL WAR TRAINING: Permanently increases the hit points of the Knight.

Priest

The Priest is a spellcaster with a ranged attack that can harm both land and air units. It comes equipped with the Heal spell, but can learn Dispel Magic and Inner Fire.

HEAL: [Autocast spell] Restores hit points to one friendly unit.

DISPEL MAGIC: Eliminates all spells on all units within an area of effect. Also damages summoned units.

INNER FIRE: [Autocast spell] Improves the attack and defense of a friendly unit.

Sorceress

The Sorceress can attack air and ground targets with its basic ranged attack, but wields powerful spells as well. It can automatically cast Slow, and can learn Invisibility and Polymorph.

SLOW: [Autocast spell] Reduces the attack and movement speed of a single enemy unit.

INVISIBILITY: Turns one friendly unit invisible for a brief duration. Invisibility ends if the unit attacks or casts a spell.

POLYMORPH: Turns an enemy unit into a sheep. The sheep retains its former hit points but loses all attacks and spells.

Gyrocopter

The airborne Gyrocopter is an effective defense against air units. It cannot initially attack land units. It can benefit from the following abilities:

GYROCOPTER BOMBS: Gives the Gyrocopter an air-to-ground attack against land units.

TRUE SIGHT: [Passive] This is an innate ability that allows the Gyrocopter to detect invisible units.

Mortar Team

The Mortar Team is a slow land unit that can attack land units, buildings, and trees with its long-range siege attack. Mortar Teams have a minimum range, so they cannot hit enemies that are next to them. The Mortar Team can learn the following ability:

FLARE: Temporarily reveals a portion of the fog of war and detects invisible units. Can be used only once.

Steam Tank

This land unit has a heavily armored hull, and a powerful attack against buildings. The Steam Tank cannot attack other units.

Gryphon Rider

The Gryphon Rider is an air unit that can attack both land and air units. It can benefit from the following upgrades:

ANIMAL WAR TRAINING: Permanently increases the hit points of the Gryphon Rider.

STORM HAMMERS: Permits the storm hammers thrown by the Gryphon Rider to strike through initial ground targets and damage those behind.

Water Elemental

The Water Elemental is a land unit summoned by the Archmage with the Summon Water Elemental spell. As the Summon Water Elemental spell is upgraded, the elemental summoned gains better attack strength and more hit points. It dissipates after a short period of time.

Buildings

Town Hall

The Town Hall is the center of any Human settlement. It is where Peasants are recruited, and where Peasants drop off their gold and lumber loads. The Town Hall buildings house the Call to Arms bell that will turn your Peasants into Militia.

Keep

You can upgrade your Town Hall to a Keep, which enables further upgrades and is harder to destroy.

Castle

You can upgrade your Keep to a Castle. The Castle is the toughest Human Town Hall and enables the highest-level of units and upgrades.

Farm

Farms provide a modest amount of food, but are quick and cheap to build.

Barracks

The Barracks is where you train Footmen, Riflemen, and Knights. Here is where you also research the Defend, Long Rifles, and Animal War Training upgrades.

Blacksmith

The Blacksmith is where the weapons and armor of Alliance troops are improved, thus enhancing their attack and defense. The attack of Militia, Footmen, Knights, Riflemen, Mortar Teams, and Gyrocopters can be upgraded here. In addition, the armor of these units, as well as the armor of Steam Tanks and Gryphon Riders, may be upgraded here.

Lumber Mill

The Lumber Mill is an alternative drop site for wood. It is also where technologies can be researched to improve Human lumber harvesting and the sturdiness of Human buildings.

Scout Tower

These towers have no attack but provide field of vision of the map. They can be upgraded into either Guard Towers or Cannon Towers.

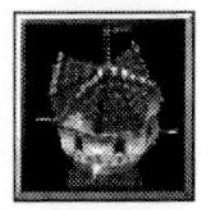

Guard Tower

Capable of attacking land and air units, the Guard Tower is an able defense for Human settlements.

Cannon Tower

The Cannon Tower is an alternative to the Guard Tower. While it can only attack ground targets and has a slower attack, it is more powerful.

Workshop

The Workshop is where Gyrocopters, Mortar Teams, and Steam Tanks are built. The Gyrocopter Bombs upgrade and the Mortar Team's Flare ability are researched here.

Arcane Sanctum

Priests and Sorceresses are trained within the mystic hallways of the Arcane Sanctum. This is also where Priests learn Dispel Magic and Inner Fire, and where Sorceresses learn Invisibility and Polymorph. The Magic Sentry upgrade, which allows your towers to detect invisible units, is also researched here.

Gryphon Aviary

The Aviary is where Gryphon Riders and their upgrade, Storm Hammers, are trained.

Altar of Kings

This building is where the Alliance recruits and revives its Heroes.

Orcish Horde

The Horde possesses the game's most powerful ground units, including the savage Grunt and gargantuan Tauren. The Orcish Horde has modest air and ranged capabilities, but their true might lies in their brute strength and raw melee power. Even the magic of their spellcasters is designed to enhance their frontline troops.

Spiked Barricades

The buildings of the Orcish Horde can be outfitted with spikes that damage all enemy melee units that attack them. There are multiple upgrades, each empowering the spikes to do more damage. The Spiked Barricades upgrades are researched at the War Mill.

Pillage

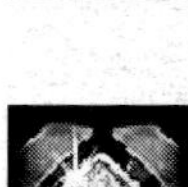

Certain Orc units can be upgraded to salvage gold and lumber when attacking enemy buildings. Once trained, Pillage enables Peons, Grunts, and Raiders to add gold to your coffers every time they hit an enemy building.

Protective Burrows

The Orcish food supply building is the Orc Burrow; however, it also doubles as a defensive structure. When garrisoned with Peons, it can provide defense against land and air units in the form of a ranged attack.

Unload Peons

Battle Stations

Orc Heroes

Blademaster

The Blademaster is an agile Hero who can attack other land units. He can learn the following abilities:

WIND WALK: Turns the Blademaster invisible for a brief time.

MIRROR IMAGE: Creates illusory copies of the Blademaster. Casting Mirror Image also removes any spell effects on the Blademaster, whether good or ill.

CRITICAL STRIKE: [Passive] Gives the Blademaster a chance of dealing extra damage with each melee attack.

BLADESTORM: [Ultimate] A whirlwind attack against all nearby enemy ground units, during which time the Blademaster is immune to spells.

Far Seer

This spellcasting Hero has a ranged attack that affects land and air targets. He can learn the following spells:

CHAIN LIGHTNING: Fires a bolt of lightning that arcs to multiple enemy targets, dealing less damage with each hit.

FAR SIGHT: Temporarily unveils a portion of the map, revealing invisible units as well.

FERAL SPIRIT: Summons two Spirit Wolves to serve the Far Seer for a limited time. The type of wolf summoned improves as the spell level is increased.

EARTHQUAKE: [Ultimate] Damages all buildings in an area of effect and slows all units caught in the area.

Tauren Chieftain

The Chieftain is the most powerful melee Hero in the game and can attack other land units. He can learn the following abilities:

SHOCKWAVE: Sends a wave of force that damages enemy land units in a short line.

WAR STOMP: Stomps the ground, stunning and damaging nearby enemy land units.

ENDURANCE AURA: [Passive] Improves the attack speed and movement speed of all nearby friendly units.

REINCARNATION: [Ultimate] [Passive] Raises your Tauren Chieftain from the dead.

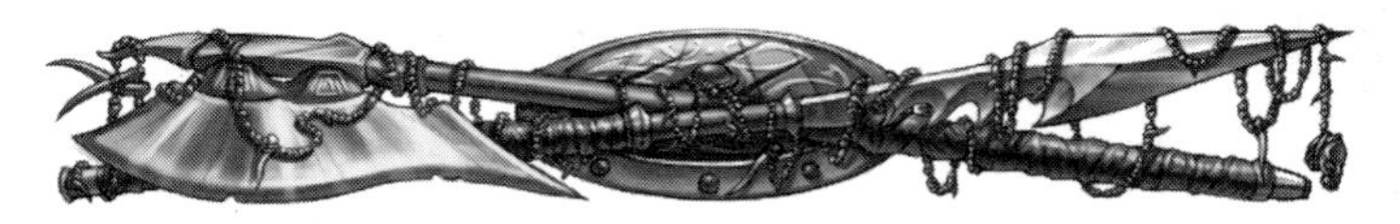

Orc Units

Peon

Peons build structures and harvest gold and lumber for the Horde.

REPAIR: [Autocast ability] Peons can repair all friendly buildings and mechanical units. They can learn the following ability:

PILLAGE: [Passive] Allows the Peon to earn gold every time it hits an enemy building.

Grunt

The Grunt is a melee unit that can attack other land units. It can learn the following abilities:

PILLAGE: [Passive] Allows the Grunt to earn gold every time it hits an enemy building.

BERSERKER STRENGTH: Increases the hit points of the Grunt.

Troll Headhunter

The Headhunter is a spear-throwing unit that can attack land and air units. Headhunters can benefit from the following ability:

TROLL REGENERATION: Increases hit point regeneration rate of the Troll Headhunter.

Catapult

This mechanical siege unit has a devastating long-range attack against buildings. It does less damage against troops, and cannot hit air units, but it can be used to quickly fell trees. Like other siege units, it has a minimum range.

Tauren

The hulking Tauren is a melee fighter that can attack other land units. It can learn the following ability:

PULVERIZE: [Passive] Gives the Tauren a chance of dealing area-effect damage to enemy ground units with each attack.

Shaman

The Shaman has a ranged attack that harms land and air units. Its beginning spell is Purge, and it can learn Lightning Shield and Bloodlust.

PURGE: Removes any spells on the target, and slows its movement speed. Also damages summoned units.

LIGHTNING SHIELD: Surrounds one unit with a shield of lightning that damages all ground units next to it. Can only be cast on ground units.

BLOODLUST: [Autocast spell] Improves the attack and movement speed of a friendly unit.

Troll Witch Doctor

The Witch Doctor is a spellcaster with a ranged attack effective against land and air units. It begins with the Sentry Ward spell, and can learn Stasis Trap and Healing Ward. It can also benefit from the Troll Regeneration ability.

SENTRY WARD: Places a long lasting invisible ward on the ground that can detect invisible units.

STASIS TRAP: Places an invisible trap on the ground that stuns any ground units in its area of effect. Air units do not trigger Stasis Trap. The trap is only triggered by enemy ground units and dissipates after discharging.

HEALING WARD: Places a temporary ward on the ground that heals all nearby friendly units.

TROLL REGENERATION: Increases hit point regeneration rate of the Witch Doctor.

Raider

Raiders are fast melee units that can attack land units. Raiders do excellent damage versus buildings. They can learn the following abilities:

ENSNARE: Throws a net over an enemy unit, immobilizing it. Melee units can attack an ensnared air unit.

PILLAGE: [Passive] Allows a unit to earn gold every time it hits an enemy building.

Kodo Beast

The Kodo Beast has a ranged attack that hits land and air units. This unit has the following abilities:

DEVOUR: The Kodo Beast can Devour a non-Hero unit, slowly digesting it. If the Kodo Beast is killed before it fully digests its meal, the enemy will burst out. The Devour ability requires no training.

WAR DRUMS: [Passive] This automatic ability of the Kodo Beast gives all nearby friendly units an attack bonus. War Drums may be upgraded to improve the attack bonus.

Wyvern

Wyverns are air units that can attack air and land units. They can learn the following ability:

ENVENOMED WEAPON: [Passive] Coats the Wyvern's attacks in poison, which deals additional damage over a period of time.

Spirit Wolf, Dire Wolf, and Shadow Wolf

The Spirit Wolf is a land unit summoned by the Far Seer with the Feral Spirit spell. Two Spirit Wolves are summoned per casting. If Feral Spirit is cast more than once, the previous wolves disappear to make way for the new wolves. As the spell is upgraded, the summoned Spirit Wolves become Dire Wolves and then Shadow Wolves. Dire Wolves are stronger, while Shadow Wolves are invisible and stronger still. All types of Spirit Wolf dissipate after a short period of time.

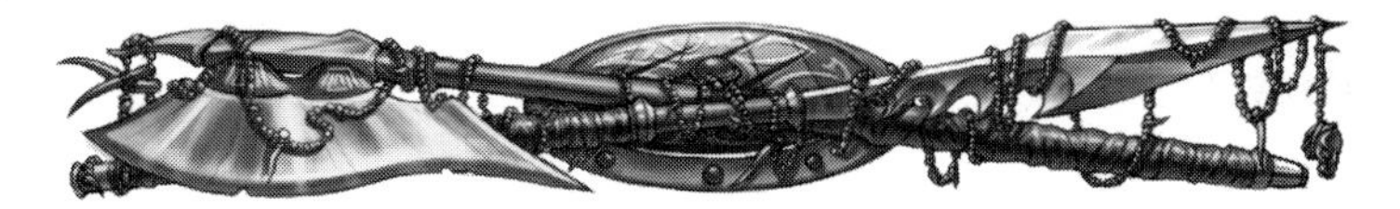

Orc Buildings

Great Hall

The Great Hall is where Orcish Peons answer the call to duty. Peons deliver their gold and lumber cargo here. The Pillage ability is researched at this Orcish "Town Hall."

Stronghold

The Great Hall can be upgraded to a Stronghold. A Stronghold is much harder to destroy and enables further upgrades to be researched.

Fortress

The Stronghold can be upgraded to a Fortress. The Fortress is the mightiest of the Orcish Town Hall buildings, and enables the highest-level upgrades for the Horde.

Orc Burrow

Burrows provide food for the Horde. They can also be garrisoned with Peons during times of trouble. Once inside, Peons will hurl spears at enemy units to protect their lands.

BATTLE STATIONS: Activating Battle Stations calls all nearby Peons to garrison themselves inside the nearest Burrows and to automatically attack incoming enemies.

Barracks

Grunts, Troll Headhunters, and Catapults are recruited at the Barracks. The Berserker Strength and Troll Regeneration upgrades are researched here.

War Mill

Orc smiths and Troll craftsmen work side by side at the War Mill to improve the weapons and armor of the Horde troops. The attack and armor upgrades researched here affect Grunts, Headhunters, Tauren, Raiders, Wyverns, and Catapults. The Spiked Barricades upgrade is also researched here.

Watch Tower

Embattled Orcish settlements can be guarded with Watch Towers, which provide static defense against land and air attacks.

Spirit Lodge

The Spirit Lodge trains Shaman and Witch Doctors. The Shaman's Lightning Shield and Bloodlust spells are researched here, as well as the Witch Doctor's Stasis Trap and Healing Ward spells.

Beastiary

The Beastiary trains Raiders, Kodo Beasts, and Wyverns. Ensnare, War Drums, and Envenomed Weapon abilities are researched here.

Altar of Storms

The Altar of Storms is where the Horde's Heroes are recruited and where they are revived if they are slain.

Tauren Totem

Tauren are trained at the Tauren Totem. The Pulverize ability is researched here.

Undead Scourge

Undead Scourge

The Undead Scourge is a well-balanced faction that can field enduring ground forces and powerful air units. Their spellcasters possess a variety of powerful magics, including the dreaded ability to raise fallen allies and foes alike into an army of walking dead. In this way, the Undead can field armies more numerous than any other race in Warcraft III.

Summoned Buildings

The Undead do not build structures, but instead summon them into being. Once an Acolyte is told to build a building, it begins the summoning spell, and the building gradually appears. During this time, the Acolyte can return to its duties, since it does not need to stay with a building while it is being summoned. The Undead can also Unsummon their buildings and recoup a percentage of the gold and lumber cost originally used to summon the building.

Blight

Most Undead buildings must be summoned on the Blight, a corrupting influence that turns the land under an Undead settlement to rotted soil. Only two buildings can be summoned on normal land: the Necropolis and a Haunted Gold Mine. Once completed, these buildings generate a radius of Blight, upon which subsequent Undead buildings can be summoned. Each additional building you summon extends the radius of Blight further.

Blight Regeneration

An Undead unit will regenerate its health faster when it is standing on, or hovering over Blight.

Corpses

In addition to gold and lumber, the Undead Scourge harvest corpses as a tertiary resource. Corpses are not used for purchasing units or raising buildings, but instead are used to fuel some of the powers of the Undead. The Necromancer unit uses corpses to create Skeleton Warriors, while the Ghoul unit consumes corpses to rapidly restore health. Corpses disappear over time, but the Undead can store them in their Meat Wagon units, where they will not decay and can be unloaded for use when the need arises.

Undead Resource Gathering

The Undead harvest resources with two units: Acolytes mine gold and Ghouls harvest lumber. In order to mine gold, Acolytes must first summon a Haunted Gold Mine over an existing mine. Then, up to five Acolytes may gather around the Haunted Gold Mine and begin adding gold to your reserves, without having to carry it back to the Necropolis. Ghouls will deposit lumber at your Necropolis or Graveyard.

Undead Heroes

Death Knight

The Death Knight is a melee unit that can attack other land targets. He can learn the following abilities:

DEATH COIL: A bolt of energy that heals friendly undead units or harms enemy living units.

DEATH PACT: Destroys an Undead unit of your choosing to restore the Death Knight's hit points.

UNHOLY AURA: [Passive] Quickens the hit point regeneration and movement speed of nearby friendly units.

ANIMATE DEAD: [Ultimate] Temporarily raises a handful of recently slain units. Friendly or hostile units can be raised, but all serve the Death Knight regardless of former allegiance.

Dread Lord

This Hero has a melee attack effective against land units, but also possesses powerful spells. He can learn the following abilities:

CARRION SWARM: Damages a cone of enemy ground units.

SLEEP: Puts an enemy unit or Hero to sleep, rendering it inert for a brief period of time.

VAMPIRIC AURA: [Passive] Allows nearby friendly melee units to regain hit points with every successful attack they make.

INFERNO: [Ultimate] Summons an Infernal demon from the sky to strike the ground, harming and stunning nearby enemy ground units. The fiery Infernal will then fight as a summoned unit for a limited time.

Lich

The Lich is a spellcasting Hero that can attack land and air units. He can learn the following spells:

FROST NOVA: Creates an explosion of frost that damages and slows one enemy unit and harms all nearby enemy units.

FROST ARMOR: Improves the armor of one friendly unit and encases it in a shield of ice that slows enemy melee attackers.

DARK RITUAL: Destroys one of your Undead units to replenish the mana of the Lich.

DEATH AND DECAY: [Ultimate] Damages all units and buildings in a large area of effect. Can destroy trees.

Undead Units

Acolyte

The Acolyte summons buildings and mines gold for the Undead. It possesses a weak melee attack that can harm other land targets. Acolytes can only repair undead buildings and friendly mechanical units. The Acolyte can be turned into a Shade once the Sacrificial Pit is summoned.

RESTORE: [Autocast spell] Allows the Acolyte to repair friendly Undead buildings and friendly mechanical units.

Shade

The Shade is an invisible unit that enters the game with the ability True Sight. It has no attack.

TRUE SIGHT: [Passive] This is a permanent ability that allows the Shade to detect invisible units.

Ghoul

The Ghoul is a melee unit that can attack other land units. The Ghoul is also the Scourge's only unit that can harvest lumber. It can learn the following abilities:

CANNIBALIZE: Allows the Ghoul to consume corpses to restore health.

GHOUL FRENZY: Enables Ghouls to move and attack more quickly.

Crypt Fiend

This durable land unit has a ranged attack that only affects land units. It can learn the following ability:

WEB: [Autocast spell] Traps one enemy air unit in a web, immobilizing it and drawing it down to the ground, where land units can attack it.

Gargoyle

The Gargoyle is an air unit that can attack land and air units. When attacking ground units, it has a ranged attack. When fighting air units, it has a melee attack. It can learn the following ability:

STONE FORM: The Gargoyle lands and transforms into a statue. During this time, it cannot attack, but it regenerates health rapidly, has heightened armor, and is immune to spells.

Meat Wagon

This mechanical siege unit can attack land units and buildings from afar, and can also clear trees. It can store corpses for later use by other Undead units. Like other siege units, it has a minimum range. It can learn the following ability at the

DISEASE CLOUD: [Passive] All units hit by a Meat Wagon are infected with a Disease Cloud, suffering additional damage over a period of time. Attacking ground with a Meat Wagon that has

Disease Cloud will disease enemy units for a short time. Undead units are immune to this ability.

Abomination

This large melee unit can attack other land units. It can learn the following ability:

DISEASE CLOUD: [Passive] All nearby enemy units suffer damage over a period of time after coming in contact with the Abomination. When the Abomination dies, it leaves behind a lingering miasma of disease that eventually dissipates. Undead units are immune to this ability.

Necromancer

The Necromancer is a ranged unit that can attack land and air targets. It starts with the Raise Dead spell, and can learn Unholy Frenzy and Cripple.

RAISE DEAD: [Autocast spell] Summons Skeleton Warriors from a corpse.

UNHOLY FRENZY: Diminishes the health of one unit but improves its attack rate.

CRIPPLE: Decreases the attack rate, movement speed, and damage of one enemy unit.

Banshee

This spellcasting unit can attack land and air units with its ranged attack. It begins play with the Curse spell, and can learn Anti-magic Shell and Possession.

CURSE: [Autocast spell] Gives one enemy unit a percentage chance to miss with each attack.

ANTI-MAGIC SHELL: Makes one unit immune to all spells.

POSSESSION: Turns one enemy land unit or creep to your side. Casting this spell destroys the Banshee. Cannot be used on powerful creeps.

Frost Wyrm

This powerful air unit has a ranged attack that can harm land and air targets. It can learn the following ability:

FREEZING BREATH: [Passive] Temporarily stops production at enemy buildings when this breath weapon hits them.

Skeleton Warrior

Skeleton Warriors are raised from corpses by the Necromancer's Raise Dead spell. Warriors will appear from a corpse, regardless of the type of creature it was in life. Skeleton Warriors are melee units that can attack other land units, but dissipate after a short period of time. This duration can be extended with the Skeleton Longevity upgrade at the Temple of the Damned.

Infernal

Infernal demons are called down from the sky by the Dread Lord's Inferno spell, causing area-effect damage where they land. They are melee units that can attack other land units. The fire that surrounds an Infernal acts as a permanent Immolation aura.

Immolation: Surrounds the unit in flames that damage all nearby enemy ground units.

Undead Buildings

Necropolis

The Necropolis is the Scourge's "Town Hall" where faithful Acolytes are recruited. It is only one of two buildings that can be built on normal land. All other Undead buildings must be placed on Blight.

Halls of the Dead

You can upgrade your Necropolis to a Halls of the Dead, which will enable further upgrades for your Scourge units and buildings. The Halls of the Dead is harder to destroy and is automatically able to attack land and air units.

Black Citadel

The Halls of the Dead can be upgraded to a Black Citadel, unlocking the highest-level upgrades for your units. The vile Black Citadel is the strongest of the Undead Town Halls and is also capable of attacking land and air units.

Haunted Gold Mine

This building must be summoned on top of a gold mine before you can begin mining gold with your Acolytes. It does not require Blight to be summoned.

Ziggurat

The Ziggurat provides food for the Undead Scourge and can also be upgraded into a defensive structure called the Spirit Tower.

Spirit Tower

The Spirit Tower has a ranged attack that affects land and air units. A Spirit Tower continues to generate food as a Ziggurat even while operating as static defense.

Crypt

This building is where you recruit Ghouls, Crypt Fiends, and Gargoyles. It is also where you research the Cannibalize, Ghoul Frenzy, Web, and Stone Form abilities.

Graveyard

The Graveyard is where Undead troops can have their attack and defenses upgraded by dark rituals. The attack and armor of Ghouls, Abominations, Skeleton Warriors, Crypt Fiends, Gargoyles, and Frost Wyrms are upgraded here. Graveyards can be a source of free corpses, because they generate corpses over time.

Slaughterhouse

The Slaughterhouse is where Meat Wagons and Abominations are created. It is also where the Disease Cloud upgrade is researched.

Temple of the Damned

Necromancers and Banshees are created at this building. The Necromancer spells, Unholy Frenzy and Cripple, are learned here, as are the Banshee spells, Anti-magic Shell and Possession. Skeleton Longevity, which increases the duration of Skeleton Warriors, is researched here as well.

Boneyard

The Boneyard is where Frost Wyrms are created. The Freezing Breath ability is also researched here.

Sacrificial Pit

This is where Acolytes are permanently turned into Shades.

Altar of Darkness

Scourge Heroes are recruited at this unholy Altar. Your fallen Heroes are revived at the Altar of Darkness.

Night Elf Sentinels

The Night Elves of Kalimdor are a mighty race that emphasizes mobility, ranged firepower, and spellcraft. They do not have the brute strength of other races, but their skills with bow and magic more than compensate for this deficiency.

Ancients

Several buildings of the Night Elves are actually sentient trees that can move. They are the Tree of Life, Tree of Ages, Tree of Eternity, Ancient of War, Ancient of Wind, Ancient of Lore, and Ancient Protector. These buildings can be uprooted with the Uproot command, and moved around at will. When walking they can attack land units, but they cannot engage in their normal activities, such as receiving resources or creating units. To return to building form, they must re-root themselves. All Ancients have the Eat Tree ability.

Ancients

Ancients can benefit from the following abilities:

EAT TREE: If damaged, Ancients can consume trees to regain health.

NATURE'S BLESSING: This ability is researched at the Tree of Eternity, and once completed improves the movement speed and armor of Ancients.

Shadowmeld

Night Elf females possess the Shadowmeld ability. This enables them to turn invisible when they are not moving or attacking. The Archer, Huntress, and Priestess of the Moon all possess this ability. To force these units to remain motionless, even when enemy units would otherwise provoke response, you may use the Hide button. Shadowmeld only operates during nighttime.

Enhanced Night Vision

Night Elves can be upgraded to see as adeptly in darkness as they do in daylight. This ability is called Ultravision, and is researched at the Hunter's Hall.

Moon Wells

The Moon Wells of the Night Elves, in addition to providing food, have mana reserves that can be used to restore the hit points and mana of nearby Night Elf units. Mana spent in this way slowly regenerates, but only at nighttime.

Night Elf Resource Gathering

In order to mine gold, Night Elves must first entangle a gold mine with their Tree of Life using the Entangle Gold Mine command. Once entangled, Wisps must then enter the mine to begin gold gathering. Up to five Wisps may remain in an Entangled Gold Mine at a time. Wisps do not need to return to a Tree of Life to deposit gold, which is automatically added to the Night Elf reserves while Wisps remain in the gold mine. To harvest lumber, Wisps bond to nearby trees, slowly adding small amounts of lumber to your reserves without harming the tree. As with gold, Wisps do not need to return to your Tree of Life to deposit wood.

Night Elf Heroes

Demon Hunter

This Hero is a melee fighter that can attack land units. He can learn the following abilities:

MANA BURN: Fires a bolt that drains mana from an enemy unit and does an equal amount of damage to the unit.

IMMOLATION: Surrounds the Demon Hunter in flames that damage all nearby enemy ground units.

EVASION: [Passive] Gives the Demon Hunter a chance to completely evade an enemy attack.

METAMORPHOSIS: [Ultimate] Transforms the Demon Hunter into a Demon, giving him bonus hit points, rapid hit point regeneration, and a ranged fireball attack.

Keeper of the Grove

The Keeper has a ranged attack that harms land and air units. He can learn the following abilities:

ENTANGLING ROOTS: Roots enemy ground units in place and deals damage to them over time.

FORCE OF NATURE: Summons Treants from trees to fight on behalf of the Keeper.

THORNS AURA: [Passive] Gives all nearby friendly units an aura that damages any melee units that attack them.

TRANQUILITY: [Ultimate] Heals all nearby friendly units.

Priestess of the Moon

The Priestess of the Moon has a ranged attack effective against both land and air units. She can use the following abilities:

HIDE: Forces your Priestess to remain motionless; she will not attack while hidden.

SCOUT: Sends an owl to reveal a location of the map for a few seconds. Can detect invisible units.

SEARING ARROWS: [Autocast spell] Adds fire damage to the Priestess' ranged attack. Will only affect enemy units.

TRUESHOT AURA: [Passive] Increases the ranged attack damage of all nearby friendly units.

STARFALL: [Ultimate] Sends waves of stars crashing around the Priestess, dealing damage to all surrounding enemy units while leaving friendly units unscathed.

Night Elf Units

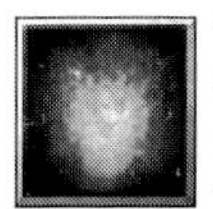

Wisp

Wisps mine gold and harvest lumber for the Night Elves. They also create the Night Elf buildings. When creating Ancients, Wisps are lost in the process. However, when creating other buildings, Wisps remain after construction is complete.

RENEW: [Autocast spell] Allows the Wisp to repair friendly Night Elf buildings and friendly mechanical units.

DETONATE: Destroys the Wisp, creating an explosion that dispels all magic in the area surrounding the Wisp. The explosion also drains mana from nearby units and damages summoned units.

Archer

The Archer is a ranged unit that can attack land and air targets. It can benefit from the following abilities:

HIDE: Forces your Archer to remain motionless; unit will not attack while hidden.

IMPROVED BOWS: Once researched, this ability permanently increases the attack range of the Archer.

MARKSMANSHIP: Once researched, this ability permanently increases the damage of the Archer.

MOUNT HIPPOGRYPH: Researched at the Ancient of Wind, this ability lets the Archer mount a Hippogryph, creating a Hippogryph Rider unit and eliminating the Archer.

Huntress

This fast-moving unit has a ranged attack that can affect land units. It can benefit from the following abilities:

HIDE: Forces your Huntress to remain motionless; unit will not attack while hidden.

SENTINEL: Sends an owl to a nearby tree to provide permanent visibility of the area, revealing any invisible units there as well. If the tree the owl rests on is cut down, the Sentinel ends. The Huntress can only use this ability once.

UPGRADE MOON GLAIVE: Allows the Huntress' attack to bounce to additional foes, doing less damage with each ricochet. The upgraded glaive will only hit ground units.

Ballista

This mechanical siege unit can attack land units and buildings. It can also destroy trees. As with other siege units, it has a minimum range. It can benefit from the following upgrade:

IMPALING BOLT: Permits the bolts launched by the Ballista to strike through initial ground targets and damage those behind.

Dryad

The Dryad has a ranged attack that can harm land and air units. It begins with Abolish Magic and can learn Slow Poison and Magic Immunity spells.

ABOLISH MAGIC: [Autocast spell] Dispels any positive spells on a single enemy unit or negative spells on a single friendly unit, and also damages summoned units.

SLOW POISON: [Passive] This ability of the Dryad requires no research. When attacked by the Dryad, even magic-immune units will be poisoned and slowed. This spell's effects cannot be dispelled.

MAGIC IMMUNITY: [Passive] Makes the Dryad immune to negative spells.

Druid of the Claw

This Druid is a melee unit that can attack other land units. It arrives from the Ancient of Lore with the ability to cast Roar. It can learn to cast the Rejuvenation and Bear Form spells.

ROAR: Improves the attack damage of nearby friendly units.

REJUVENATION: Heals the hit points of one friendly unit.

BEAR FORM: Changes the Druid to Bear Form and back. The Druid can only cast spells while in Night Elf Form. In Bear Form, it can only make melee attacks, but has a stronger attack and more hit points.

Druid of the Talon

This Druid has a ranged attack that can affect land and air units. It arrives from the Ancient of Wind with the ability to cast Faerie Fire and can learn the Storm Crow Form and Cyclone spells.

FAERIE FIRE: [Autocast spell] Reduces the armor of a target enemy unit and provides vision of that unit.

CYCLONE: Summons a cyclone to stun one enemy unit.

STORM CROW FORM: Transforms the Druid into a storm crow and back. The Druid can only cast spells while in Night Elf Form. In Storm Crow Form, it possesses a ranged attack that affects air units only.

Hippogryph

This air unit has a melee attack that affects other air units only. Once the Hippogryph Taming ability is researched at the Ancient of Wind, an Archer can mount the Hippogryph, creating a Hippogryph Rider unit. It can benefit from the following upgrade:

PICK UP ARCHER: When Hippogryph Taming is researched at the Ancient of Wind, this ability lets the Hippogryph be mounted by an Archer, creating a Hippogryph Rider unit and eliminating the Hippogryph.

Hippogryph Rider

This air unit is created when an Archer mounts a Hippogryph. The Hippogryph Rider has a ranged attack that can hit land and air targets.

Chimaera

This air unit can hit land and air units with its ranged attack. It can learn the following ability:

CORROSIVE BREATH: [Passive] A passive ability that spits a glob of acid on a building.

Treant

The Keeper of the Grove summons this unit with the Force of Nature spell. The spell destroys a few trees and creates a Treant. This unit has a melee attack that affects land units. Treants do not get stronger as the Force of Nature spell is upgraded. Instead, upgraded Force of Nature spells summon additional Treants. Each Treant dissipates after a brief period of time.

Night Elf Buildings

Tree of Life

The Tree of Life is where Wisps are created and acts as a Town Hall for the Night Elf Sentinels. Wisps do not need to return here to drop off gold and lumber, but the Tree must be rooted in order to receive gold.

Tree of Ages

You can upgrade your Tree of Life to a Tree of Ages. A Tree of Ages enables you to research further upgrades and is harder to destroy than the basic Tree of Life.

Tree of Eternity

The final upgrade to this Night Elf Town Hall is the Tree of Eternity. The Tree of Eternity enables research of the highest-level upgrades and units. The Tree of Eternity is also the strongest of the mighty Ancients.

Moon Well

Moon Wells provide food for the Night Elves, but can also replenish mana and health to friendly units. Mana in a Moon Well is regenerated during nighttime.

Ancient of War

The Ancient of War is where Archers, Huntresses, and Ballistae are created. The Sentinel, Improved Bows, Marksmanship Upgrade Moon Glaive, and Impaling Bolt abilities are researched here.

Hunter's Hall

The Hunter's Hall is where the arrows and armor of Night Elf units are upgraded. The attack of Archers, Huntresses, Ballistae, Hippogryphs, Hippogryph Riders, Druids of the Claw and Talon, and Chimaeras are upgraded here. The armor of those units, with the exception of the Ballistae, can also be upgraded at the Hunter's Hall. Ultravision, which extends Night Elf night vision, is also researched here.

Ancient Protector

The Ancient Protector is the defensive structure for the Night Elves. It can attack land or air units with its ranged attack.

Ancient of Lore

This Ancient is where Dryads and Druids of the Claw are created. The Dryad's Magic Immunity and the Druid of the Claw's Rejuvenation and Bear Form spells are researched here.

Ancient of Wind

The Ancient of Wind is where Hippogryphs and Druids of the Talon are recruited. The Druid of the Talon's spells, Storm Crow Form and Cyclone, are researched here, as is Hippogryph Taming.

Chimaera Roost

The Chimaera Roost is where Chimaeras are trained. It is also where the Chimaera's Corrosive Breath ability is researched.

Altar of Elders

Night Elf Heroes are recruited and revived at the Altar of Elders.

Humans: the Alliance of Lordaeron

Human History

(SINCE THE END OF THE SECOND WAR)

Aftermath of the Second War

The devastating Second War against the orcish horde left the Alliance of Lordaeron in a state of shock and disarray. The bloodthirsty orcs, led by the mighty warchief, Orgrim Doomhammer, not only smashed their way through the dwarf-held lands of Khaz Modan, but had razed many of Lordaeron's central provinces as well. The unrelenting orcs even succeeded in ravaging the elves' remote kingdom of Quel'Thalas before their rampage was finally stopped. The Alliance armies led by Sir Anduin Lothar, Uther the Lightbringer, and Admiral Daelin Proudmoore pushed the orcs south into the shattered land of Azeroth – the first kingdom to fall before the orcs' ruthless onslaught.

The Alliance forces under Sir Lothar managed to push Doomhammer's clans out of Lordaeron and back into the orc-controlled lands of Azeroth. Lothar's forces surrounded the orcs' volcanic citadel of Blackrock Spire and laid siege to their defenses. In a last-ditch effort, Doomhammer and his lieutenants staged a daring charge from the Spire and clashed with Lothar's paladins in the center of the Burning Steppes. Doomhammer and Lothar squared off in a titanic battle that left both mighty combatants battered and drained. Though Doomhammer narrowly succeeded in vanquishing Lothar, the great hero's death did not have the effect the warchief had hoped for.

Turalyon, Lothar's most trusted lieutenant, took up Lothar's bloodstained shield and rallied his grief-stricken brethren for a vicious counterattack. Under the ragged standards of both Lordaeron and Azeroth, Turalyon's troops slaughtered the bulk of Doomhammer's remaining forces in a glorious, but terrible rout. There was nothing left for the ragged, scattered orc survivors but to flee to the last standing bastion of orcish power – the dark portal.

Turalyon and his warriors chased the remaining orcs through the festering Swamp of Sorrows and into the corrupted Blasted Lands where the dark portal stood. There, at the foot of the colossal portal, the broken horde and the rugged Alliance clashed in what would be the last, bloodiest battle of the Second War. Outnumbered and driven mad by the curse of their bloodlust, the orcs inevitably fell before the wrath of the Alliance. Doomhammer was taken prisoner and escorted to Lordaeron while his broken clans were rounded up and hauled north - back to Lordaeron.

Beyond the Dark Portal

Only a few months after Nethergarde's completion, the energies of the dark portal coalesced and opened up a new gateway to Draenor. The remaining orc clans, under the leadership of the elder shaman, Ner'zhul, charged forth into Azeroth once again. Intent on stealing a number of magical artifacts that would increase Ner'zhul's power, the orcs planned to open up new portals in Draenor that would allow them to escape their doomed red world forever.

Convinced that Ner'zhul was planning a new offensive against the Alliance, King Terenas of Lordaeron sent his armies into Draenor to end the orcish threat once and for all. Led by Khadgar and General Turalyon, the Alliance forces clashed with the orcs across the burning landscape. Even with the aid of the elven Ranger Alleria, the dwarf Kurdran and the veteran soldier Danath, Khadgar was unable to prevent Ner'zhul from opening his portals to other worlds.

The tremendous magical storms caused by the portals' converging energies began to tear the ravaged world apart. Ner'zhul, followed only by his most trusted servants, managed to escape through one of the portals as Khadgar fought desperately to return his comrades to Azeroth. Realizing that they would be trapped on the dying world, Khadgar and his companions selflessly decided to destroy the dark portal so that Azeroth would not be harmed by Draenor's violent destruction. By all accounts, the heroes were successful in destroying the portal and saving Azeroth – but whether or not they escaped the death throes of Draenor remains to be seen.

The Battle of Grim Batol

After the destruction of the second dark portal, the Alliance succeeded in rounding up most of the renegade orc clans still left in Azeroth. The orc internment camps, built shortly after the Second War, were filled to capacity and guarded around the clock. Though the newly arrived Warsong clan had so far escaped the Alliance's wrath, there was only one group – the Dragonmaw clan – that was large enough and strong enough to upset the delicate peace that had settled over Lordaeron.

The Dragonmaw clan, led by the insidious warlock, Nekros, had conquered and held a great portion of northern Khaz Modan using dragons and small units of foot soldiers. Nekros maintained his hold over the Dragonqueen, Alexstrasza, and her red dragonflight by use of a powerful artifact known as the Demon Soul. Based in the ancient dwarven stronghold of Grim Batol, Nekros built up a sizeable army and planned to reunite the failing horde. But, despite the warlock's power, the intervention of the reckless mage, Rhonin, threw Nekros' plans awry. Rhonin and his companions, aided by

dwarven resistance fighters, succeeded in destroying the Demon Soul and freeing Alexstrasza from the orcs' control. The vengeful red dragons incinerated the Dragonmaw clan and effectively put an end to the last bastion of orcish power in the world.

With the death of Nekros, the last of the orcish warlocks – the orcs left to wallow in the crowded internment camps – slipped into a crippling lethargy. Stripped of their will to fight or even die, the orcs lost all sense of themselves as warriors – and the last traces of the proud culture that had birthed them.

The Alliance Splinters

In the years following the horde's defeat, the leaders of the various Alliance nations began to bicker and argue over territorial holdings and decreasing political influence. King Terenas of Lordaeron, the patron of the Alliance, began to suspect that the fragile pact they had forged during their darkest hour would not stand for long. Terenas had convinced the Alliance leaders to lend money and laborers to help rebuild the city of Stormwind that was destroyed during the orcish occupation of Azeroth. Those taxes, coupled with the high expense of maintaining and operating the numerous orc internment camps, led many leaders – Genn Greymane of Gilneas in particular - to believe that their kingdoms would be better off seceding from the Alliance.

To make matters worse, the brusque high elves of Silvermoon rescinded their allegiance to the Alliance, stating that the humans' poor leadership led to the burning of their forests during the Second War. Though Terenas tactfully reminded the elves that nothing of Quel'Thalas would have remained if not for the hundreds of valiant humans who'd given their lives to defend it, the elves stubbornly decided to go their own way. In the wake of the elves' departure, Gilneas and Stromgarde pulled stake and seceded as well.

Though the Alliance was falling apart, King Terenas still had allies that he could count on. Both Admiral Proudmoore of Kul Tiras and the young King, Varian Wrynn of Azeroth, remained committed to the Alliance. Also, the wizards of the Kirin Tor, led by the Archmage Antonidas, pledged Dalaran's steadfast support to Terenas' rule. Most pleasingly, perhaps, was the pledge of the mighty dwarven King, Magni Bronzebeard, who vowed that the dwarves of Ironforge would forever owe a debt of honor to the Alliance for liberating Khaz Modan from the horde's control.

A New Generation

Years passed as tensions abated and a lasting peace settled over Lordaeron. King Terenas and the Archbishop Alonsus Faol worked ceaselessly to rebuild the kingdom and bring aid to the remaining nations of the Alliance. The southern kingdom of Azeroth grew prosperous again and reestablished itself as a military power under King Wrynn's visionary leadership. Uther the Lightbringer, the supreme commander of the Paladin Order, kept the peace in Lordaeron by settling civil disputes and quelling demi-human uprisings throughout the realm. Admiral Proudmoore, whose mighty fleets patrolled the trade lanes hunting pirates and marauders, maintained order on the high seas. But it was the exploits of a newer generation of heroes that captured the imagination of the populace.

King Terenas' only son, Arthas, had grown into a strong, confident young man. The young Prince was trained as a warrior by Muradin Bronzebeard – brother to King Magni of Ironforge – and despite his youth, was considered to be one of the finest swordsmen in Lordaeron. At the tender age of nineteen Arthas was inducted into the Order of the Silver Hand under the command of Lord Uther. The kindly Uther, who had been like a brother to King Terenas for years, considered the Prince more of a favored nephew than a pupil. Though headstrong and somewhat arrogant, none could dispute Arthas' bravery and tenacity. When the troll warbands of Zul'Aman began raiding the settlements along the Quel'Thalassian border, Arthas was quick to hunt down the savages and put an end to their rampage.

Yet despite his heroics, the citizenry of Lordaeron obsessed over the young Prince's personal life. Rumors of a budding romance between Arthas and Lady Jaina Proudmoore had surfaced and set the kingdom ablaze. Jaina was the youngest daughter of Admiral Proudmoore, a childhood friend of Arthas. However, the beautiful, yet shy young woman was also the star pupil of the Kirin Tor – the Wizard Council of Dalaran. Tutored by the revered Archmage, Antonidas, Jaina was heralded as a prodigy and excelled at magical research and investigation. Despite the rigors of their duties, Arthas and Jaina managed to maintain a close relationship. Given King Terenas' age and deteriorating health, the citizenry was pleased to see that their beloved Prince would marry and carry on the royal bloodline.

Embarrassed by the public attention, Arthas and Jaina kept their affair as private as possible. But Jaina, committed to her studies in Dalaran, knew that their romance could not last. She had studied the ways of magic her whole life and knew that her true calling was the pursuit of knowledge – not the trappings of the throne room. Much to the frustration of Lordaeron's citizenry, the two lovers reluctantly parted ways and refocused themselves on their duties.

The Shadows Return

After nearly thirteen years of peace, the rumors of war began to circulate once again. The King's agents reported that a young, upstart warchief had arisen and rallied the few remaining orc clans into an elite fighting force. The young warchief was intent on tearing down the internment camps and freeing his people from their bondage. The "new horde" as it was dubbed, had brazenly attacked the northern city of Stratholme in an attempt to rescue one of its captured warriors. The horde even destroyed Durnholde – the fortress that oversaw the security of the internment camps – and murdered the officers who ran it. King Terenas sent Uther and his paladins to quell the warchief's uprising, but the crafty orcs could never be found. The young warchief proved to be something of a tactical genius – and evaded Uther's best efforts to corral his hit and run attacks.

Amidst the strain of the new orc uprising, King Terenas was disturbed to hear ill news on another front. Rumor held that a number of supposed "death cults" had formed in the northern provinces. The cults attracted the disenfranchised and disheartened citizens of Lordaeron, offering them "eternal life" on earth as an alternative to servitude to the King. After many years of peace and quiet, King Terenas knew that troubles were only just beginning for his land. He took some comfort in the fact that Lordaeron had endured every trial that had ever come its way – and that its defenders, both new and old, would see it safely through to a new dawn...

Human Hero Units

Paladin

The Archbishop, Alonsus Faol, prior to the Second War, founded the Order of the Knights of the Silver Hand. The holy knights, or paladins, as they are commonly called, led the battle against the evil orcs and helped to save the lands of Lordaeron from ruin. Though it has been nearly fifteen years since the end of the Second War, the paladins still work selflessly to protect humanity from the gnawing jaws of evil. Empowered by the Light, these mighty warriors brandish both their warhammers and holy fire in the battle against all who would trample the meek and innocent.

HOLY LIGHT

By channeling the positive energies of the Light, paladins can form a wave of healing energy to mend their comrades' wounds. This holy energy is also capable of causing damage to the undead and their dark masters.

DIVINE SHIELD

Empowered by the Light, paladins can surround themselves with an impenetrable barrier of positive energy. While they are encased in it, physical and magical attacks cannot do them any harm.

DEVOTION AURA

The mere presence of a powerful paladin can instill great courage and inner strength in those around them. This powerful, spiritual surge actually increases the defensive capabilities of those gathered near the paladin.

RESURRECTION

By invoking the grandeur of the Light, mighty paladins can bring recently slain comrades back to life – enabling them to fight on for justice, freedom and the glory of Lordaeron.

Archmage

Hailing from the magical kingdom of Dalaran, the Archmagi represent the pinnacle of magical power. Weaving their intricate enchantments, these crotchety old wizards defend humanity with all the magical powers at their disposal. Mounted atop their trusty unicorn steeds, the Archmagi brandish magical blades and ancient staves that serve to channel their fierce energies in battle. Though gruff and slightly aloof, these experienced wizards are a heartening sight upon any battlefield where the fate of humanity lies in peril.

BLIZZARD

One of the Alliance's most feared spells, Blizzard has become even more effective and deadly since its original inception during the First War. Calling down shards of freezing ice to batter and rend their enemies, Archmagi have been known to route entire armies using this spell.

SUMMON WATER ELEMENTAL

By use of this spell an Archmage can summon and control a powerful elemental comprised of water and air vapors. These creatures, capable of hurling torrents of rock-solid water at their enemies, cannot remain in the physical world for long. Thus, after a short length of time, they will vanish and return to their base liquid forms.

BRILLIANCE AURA

Some Archmagi are so powerful that their very presence enhances the energies of the spellcasters around them. These magical synergies manifest in an aura of brilliance, which increases the younger spellcasters' energy pools so that they can cast spells more often.

MASS TELEPORT

This extremely powerful spell allows the Archmage to teleport himself and his army to any friendly units or buildings in the world. However, due to the delicate nature of Mass Teleport, Archmagi can only teleport to places where someone they know currently is.

Mountain King

The mountain kings, or 'Thanes' as they are known in Ironforge, are the mightiest dwarven warriors of Khaz Modan. Wielding both

enchanted warhammers and battle-axes, these fierce fighters live to test themselves against worthy opponents. Unconcerned with their race's preoccupation with mechanical devices and the mining precious minerals, mountain kings live only for battle. Dedicated to safeguarding the Alliance that saved their kingdom during the Second War, the mountain kings can be counted upon to rally behind any banner that stands between freedom and the ever-looming shadow of evil.

STORM BOLT

The dwarves of the Aerie Peaks often practice hurling hammers, for sport and for war. But, only the mountain kings of Ironforge can hurl a hammer so hard that it stuns their enemies senseless. Thus, the Storm Bolt is one of the most dangerous and powerful attacks of the mighty mountain kings.

THUNDER CLAP

First used by Murgen Hammerfall to decimate a swathe of invading gnolls in the Alterac Mountains, this powerful ability allows the mountain kings to slam the ground and cause destructive shockwaves of energy to damage their nearby enemies.

BASH

Mountain kings who learn the Bash technique strike with such fury that their normal attacks can often stun and crush an enemy.

AVATAR

By focusing the energies of the dwarves' "newly discovered enchanted heritage", the mountain kings can grow in size and strength – and take on the physical characteristics of carved stone. In this form, they are impervious to magical attacks and have greatly increased durability.

Human Units

Peasant

Peasants are the hard-working and stouthearted citizens of Lordaeron. They serve as the backbone of the Alliance by mining the gold and harvesting lumber necessary to build up Lordaeron's military defense forces. Roused by the tales of the orcs' atrocities during the Second War, the peasants have learned to use both pick and axe to defend their communities if threatened.

CALL TO ARMS

Peasants of the Alliance have the ability to arm themselves at any town hall so that they can better fight off invading armies. Though the peasants are capable of saving their towns from surprise attacks on their towns, they are always glad to give up their weapons and go back to their regular duties.

Footman

The vast ranks of the Alliance armies have been replenished since the devastating battles of the Second war. Trained in the arts of swordsmanship, the stoic

Footmen of the Alliance serve as Lordaeron's first line of defense. Armed with broadswords and heavy kite shields, footmen are capable of breaking any enemy charge.

DEFEND
By placing their shields at a precise angle and bearing down against oncoming opponents, footmen can deflect incoming fire from enemy piercing attackers. Though this tactic does slow the footman's movement, it is an invaluable skill when employed against piercing attackers.

Knight

Though the hearty knights of Azeroth were destroyed during the First War, the shining knights of Lordaeron still continue to serve amongst the warriors of the Alliance. Wading into combat astride their noble warhorses, the knights are renowned for cutting bloody swathes through enemy ranks. The knights' speed and mobility mark them as some of the most versatile warriors of the Alliance.

Priest

Despite the high elves' official departure from the Alliance, some elves still remain true to their former human and dwarven allies. The altruistic priests of Quel'Thalas refused to abandon their roles as healers and agreed to remain in Lordaeron despite the edicts from their reclusive masters in Silvermoon. The high elven priests use their Light-given powers to heal the wounded and bolster the spirits of Lordaeron's fighting elite.

INNER FIRE
The mages of Dalaran discovered a way to bring out the potential of the warrior's fighting spirit and essentially wreathe them in their own spiritual energies. This has had the overall effect of making the Alliance warriors more resistant to damage and better able to deal damage.

DISPEL MAGIC
Many wars have been turned by this simple spell that allows priests to counter the spells of some of the most accomplished wizards. While not necessarily flashy, this spell's effects should never be underestimated.

HEAL
The positive energies of the Light can be channeled to create a healing energy wave. This technique, developed first by the high elves, and later taught to humans, has remained relatively unchanged since its original discovery.

Sorceress

As with the elven priests, the elven sorceresses who remained in Lordaeron paid little heed to their race's departure from the Alliance. These female magic users, serving as agents to the Kirin Tor of Dalaran, use their arcane powers to aid the Alliance in times of peril. Although their powers are not always used directly in combat, the sorceresses are able to aid their comrades with a wide array of specialized conjurings and magical effects.

SLOW

The Kirin Tor has developed a technique that envelops a person in a field that reduces kinetic energy. This spell actually pulls the energy directly from the creature trying to move and attack, and channels it into the ground, causing the creature to have reduced attack and movement speeds.

INVISIBILITY

This form of illusion has come back into widespread use since the days of the Second War. It creates a magical field around a person that does not impede the passing of light. Thus, normal people simply see directly through the invisible person. However, any attempts to attack or cast spells while invisible will cause the invisibility to dissipate.

POLYMORPH

Long ago, this spell was considered to be the ultimate insult to the enemy. It has the ability to turn any enemy into a mere sheep for a limited duration of time.

Water Elemental

One of the Archmage's greatest powers is his ability to summon mighty Water elementals to aid his comrades in combat. These mindless, hulking forms of water can take massive punishment from enemy units while delivering tremendous blows in return. Water elementals were a favorite tool of the Conjurors of Azeroth during the First War, and now the enchanted creatures have come to aid the defenders of freedom once again.

Mortar Team

Armed with their innovative exploding shells, the stalwart mortar teams of Ironforge are capable of blasting apart enemy ranks from long range. These fearless dwarves are masters of explosive devices and relish in pounding fortified enemy emplacements to dust.

FLARE

The flare is a chemically charged shell that, when fired by a dwarven mortar team, can reveal areas and enemies that are difficult to see, or otherwise cloaked by invisibility or Shadowmeld.

Rifleman

The brave dwarven Riflemen have faithfully protected their mountain kingdom of Khaz Modan ever since the battle of Grim Batol. Yet, as new threats arose to threaten their hard-won freedom, they offered their expert skills and tenacity to the Alliance. Using the legendary single-shot Blunderbuss Long Rifles, riflemen are excellent marksmen and can shoot both land based and airborne opponents.

Gyrocopter

The ingenious dwarven engineers, taking a nod from their inventive gnomish cousins, constructed the ultimate airborne scout vehicle. The gyrocopters are small but versatile flying machines that can cover great distances at speed and evade enemy ground forces. Though the contraptions are somewhat rickety, they are armed with mounted cannons and bombs, and piloted by the daring – if not insane – dwarven pilot corps.

Steam Tank

These cumbersome, heavily armored vehicles are mobile siege weapons piloted by brave and sometimes reckless dwarves. Their heavy weaponry is too cumbersome to target enemy units and can only be used on buildings.

Gryphon Rider

The daring dwarves of the Wildhammer clan have responded once again to the call and brought the mighty gryphons of the Aerie Peaks to aid the Alliance in its time of need. Armed with their trusty, lightning-powered Stormhammers, the fearless wild dwarves seek to keep the skies of Lordaeron free from enemy forces. The proud gryphons share their riders' implacable resolve and stand as noble symbols of the Alliance's fortitude.

Human Structures

Town Hall

The town hall is the nerve center of any human community and serves as the primary exchange for gold. It is also a center for training loyal peasants in their particular vocations, whether it be lumber harvesting, building construction, or gold mining. In time the town hall can be upgraded to stronger fortifications.

Farm

Vital to any human Village, the Farm provides sustenance for troops and citizens. The uncanny ability of these skilled farmers to harvest almost any landscape under the harshest conditions is highly regarded in the lands of Lordaeron. The number of troops sustainable at any village is dependent upon the amount of land harvested by the small farms.

Barracks

The barracks are the staging area and bunking quarters for most human troops. It is within the barracks' walls that footmen are taught the art of shield defense. Here, dwarves and humans train side by side, united by the threat of their common enemy.

Scout Tower

Scout towers may be constructed at almost any location to provide continuous on-site observation. The towers are also the first necessary step in human town defense. These structures may later be upgraded to guard or cannon towers.

MAGICAL SENTRY

This enhancement is used to allow towers to see units that are invisible. Everything seen through the sentry's effect is much sharper and more vibrant than what the naked eye can perceive.

Guard Tower

These brick towers provide the first line of defense against enemy invasion. The arrows that fly from these bastions are renowned for their deadly accuracy.

Cannon Tower

With the study and understanding of gunpowder, scout towers may be modified to house cannon. The artillery provides increased bombardment of attacking forces, limited only by the restriction of being unable to attack flying invaders. Rows of these sturdy towers provide a formidable defense against even the most aggressive assaults.

Blacksmith

At the blacksmith, the dwarves refine their mastery of gunpowder. It is also at this building where more effective steel-forging methods are researched and perfected. Human troops depend upon the blacksmith to provide both increasingly effective weapon blades and more impenetrable plates of armor.

Lumber Mill

The master masons of the human lumber mills strive constantly to improve structural integrity. The site is also a processing mill for lumber harvested from the surrounding landscape. The wood harvested is used in everything from raw building materials to weapon handles.

Workshop

The Workshop is a hideaway where dwarven smiths labor amid smoke and steel to create their unique innovations. Flying gyrocopters are assembled at this location, as well as heavily armored steam tanks. Artillery is thoroughly researched here, providing ammunition for the mobile dwarven mortar teams.

Keep

With the advancement of human technology and the need to support growing numbers of fighting troops, the town hall may be upgraded to a keep. In addition to adding heavier fortification, the keep allows for the introduction of the mage class into human society. The keep can later be upgraded even further, to a Castle.

Arcane Sanctum

Tutored in the Halls of Magic at the mystical city of Dalaran, sorceresses and priests diligently study their mysterious arts within the depths of the arcane sanctum. Over time, continuous study provides additional reserves of mana and the mastering of ever more difficult spells. It is also here that magical sentries may be called to allow the human towers to detect invisible enemy invaders.

Altar of Kings

Made from materials provided by the Kirin Tor, the Altar of Kings acts as a harness for the derelict life forces of fallen human champions. It is only at this site, once erected, that heroes may be resurrected to do battle once again. The specifics of this building's magical properties are among the most guarded secrets in all the human realms.

Castle

Castles represent the pinnacle of advanced human civilization. With this advancement comes the ability to support stables for housing the war-steeds of the heroic knights. This progression also allows the building of gryphon aviaries.

Gryphon Aviary

The greatest achievement to come from the alliance of dwarves and humans is quite possibly the taming and training of the mighty, noble Gryphons. Following years of failed attempts, dwarven riders finally succeeded in gaining the trust of the aloof Gryphons. Together with the humans, dwarven riders gave the greatest care, providing lodgings that would most closely resemble the Gryphons' aeries among Lordaeron's Aerie Peaks.

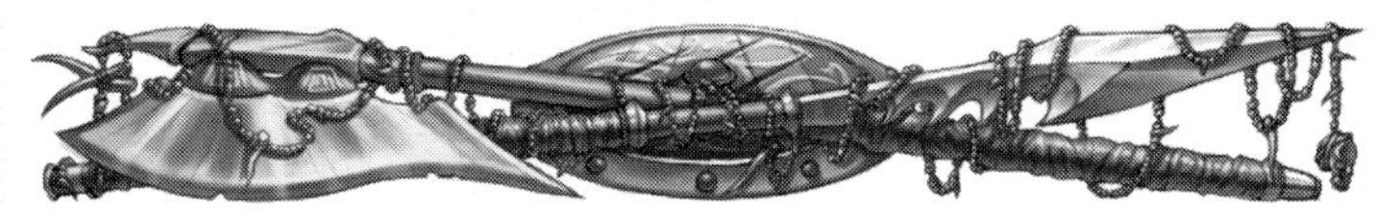

Orcs: the Horde

Orcish History

(SINCE THE END OF THE SECOND WAR)

Gul'dan and the Betrayal

During the final days of the Second War, as the horde's victory over the Alli'ance seemed almost assured, a terrible feud erupted between the two most powerful orcs on Azeroth. The nefarious warlock, Gul'dan, master of the clandestine Shadow Council, led a number of renegade clans against the might of Orgrim Doomhammer, the warchief of the horde. As Doomhammer prepared his final assault against the Capital City of Lordaeron, an assault that would have crushed the last remnants of the Alliance, Gul'dan and his renegade clans abandoned their posts and set out to sea. The bewildered Doomhammer, having lost nearly half of his standing forces to Gul'dan's treachery, was forced to pull back and forsake his greatest chance at victory over the Alliance.

The power-hungry Gul'dan, obsessed with obtaining godhood itself, set out on a desperate search for the undersea Tomb of Sargeras that he believed held the secrets of ultimate power. Having already doomed his fellow orcs to become the slaves of the Burning Legion, Gul'dan thought nothing of his supposed duty to Doomhammer. Backed by the Stormreaver and Twilight's Hammer clans, Gul'dan succeeded in raising the Tomb of Sargeras from the sea floor. However, when he opened the ancient, flooded vault, he found only crazed demons awaiting him.

Seeking to punish the wayward orcs for their costly betrayal, Doomhammer sent his forces to kill Gul'dan and bring the renegades back into the fold. For his recklessness, Gul'dan was torn apart by the maddened demons he had set loose. With their leader dead, the renegade clans quickly fell before Doomhammer's enraged legions. Though the rebellion had been quelled, the horde was unable to recoup the terrible losses it had suffered. Gul'dan's betrayal had afforded the Alliance not only hope, but also time to regroup... and retaliate.

Lord Lothar, seeing that the horde was fracturing from within, gathered the last of his forces and pushed the horde south, back into the shattered heartland of his homeland, Azeroth. There, the Alliance forces trapped the retreating horde within their volcanic fortress of Blackrock Spire.

Though Lord Lothar fell in battle at the Spire's base, his lieutenant, Turalyon, rallied the Alliance forces at the eleventh hour and pushed the horde back into the abysmal Swamp of Sorrows. Turalyon's forces succeeded in destroying the dark portal, the mystical gateway that connected the orcs to their dark, red homeworld of Draenor. Cut off from its reinforcements in Draenor and fractured by incessant infighting, the horde finally buckled in upon itself and fell before the might of the Alliance forces.

The scattered orc clans were quickly rounded up and placed within guarded internment camps. Though it seemed that the horde had been defeated for good, some remained highly skeptical that peace would last. Khadgar, the former apprentice of Medivh, convinced the Alliance high command to build the fortress of Nethergarde that would watch over the ruins of the dark portal and ensure that there would be no further invasions from Draenor.

Ner'zhul and the Shadow Clans

As the fires of the Second War died down, the Alliance took aggressive steps to contain the orcish threat. A number of large internment camps, meant to house the captive orcs, were constructed in southern Lordaeron. Guarded by both the paladins and the veteran soldiers of the Alliance, the camps proved to be a great success. Though the captive orcs were tense and anxious to do battle once more, the various camp wardens, based at the old prison-fortress of Durnholde, kept the peace and maintained a strong semblance of order.

However, on the hellish world of Draenor, a new orcish army prepared to strike at the unsuspecting Alliance. The elder shaman, Ner'zhul – the former mentor of Gul'dan – rallied the handful of clans still left on Draenor under his dark banner. Ner'zhul planned to open a number of portals on Draenor that would lead the horde to new, unspoiled worlds. To power his new portals, Ner'zhul needed a number of enchanted artifacts from Azeroth. To procure them, Ner'zhul reopened the dark portal and sent his ravenous clans charging through it.

The new horde, led by veteran chieftains such as Grom Hellscream of the Warsong clan, and Kilrogg Deadeye of the Bleeding Hollow clan, surprised the Alliance defense forces and rampaged through the countryside. Under Ner'zhul's surgical command, the orcs quickly rounded up the artifacts that they needed and fled back to the safety of Draenor.

King Terenas of Lordaeron, convinced that the orcs were preparing a new invasion of Azeroth, assembled his most trusted lieutenants. He ordered General Turalyon and the mage, Khadgar, to lead an expedition through the dark portal to put an end to the orcish threat once and for all. Turalyon and Khadgar's forces marched into

Draenor and repeatedly clashed with Ner'zhul's clans upon the ravaged Hellfire Peninsula. Though neither side gained ground, it was clear that Ner'zhul would not be stopped from completing his nefarious plans.

Ner'zhul succeeded in opening his portals to other worlds – but he did not foresee the terrible price he would pay. The portals' tremendous energies began to tear the very fabric of Draenor apart. As Turalyon's forces fought desperately to return home to Azeroth, the world of Draenor began to buckle in upon itself. Grom Hellscream and Kilrogg Deadeye, realizing that Ner'zhul's mad plans would doom their entire race, rallied the remaining orcs and escaped back to the relative safety of Azeroth. As Hellscream and Deadeye hacked their way through the human ranks in a desperate bid for freedom, the dark portal suddenly exploded behind them. For them, and the remaining orcs on Azeroth, there would be no going back... .

Ner'zhul and his Shadowmoon clan passed through their newly created portals, as massive volcanic eruptions began to break Draenor's continents apart. The burning seas rose up and roiled the shattered landscape as the tortured world was finally consumed in an apocalyptic explosion.

Day of the Dragon

Though Grom Hellscream and his Warsong clan managed to evade capture, Deadeye and his Bleeding Hollow clan were rounded up and placed in the internment camps in Lordaeron. Yet, despite the costly uprising, the camps' wardens soon re-established control over their brutish charges.

However, unknown to the Alliance's agents, a large force of orcs still roamed free in the northern wastes of Khaz Modan. The Dragonmaw clan, led by the infamous Warlock, Nekros, had maintained its control over the Dragonqueen, Alexstrasza, and her Dragonflight by using an ancient artifact known as the Demon Soul. With the Dragonqueen as his hostage, Nekros built up a secret army within the abandoned dwarf stronghold of Grim Batol. Planning to unleash his forces and the mighty red dragons on the Alliance, Nekros hoped to reunite the horde and continue its conquest of Azeroth. Yet, a small group of resistance fighters, led by the human mage, Rhonin, managed to destroy the Demon Soul and free the Dragonqueen from Nekros' command.

In their fury, Alexstrasza's dragons tore apart Grim Batol and incinerated the greater bulk of the Dragonmaw clan. Nekros' grand schemes of reunification came crashing down as the Alliance troops rounded up the remaining orc survivors and threw them into the waiting internment camps. The Dragonmaw clan's defeat signaled the end of the horde – and the end of the orcs' furious bloodlust.

Lethargy and Internment

As the months passed, more orc prisoners were rounded up and placed within the internment camps. As the camps began to overflow, the Alliance was forced to construct new camps in the plains of south of the Alterac Mountains. To properly maintain and supply the growing number of camps, King Terenas levied a new tax on the Alliance nations. This tax, as well as increased political tensions over border disputes, created widespread dissention amongst the leaders of the Alliance. It seemed that the fragile pact that had forged the human nations together in their darkest hour would break at any given moment.

Amidst the political turmoil, many of the camp wardens began to notice an unsettling change come over their orc captives. The orcs' efforts to escape from the camps or even fight amongst themselves had greatly decreased in frequency over time. The orcs were becoming increasingly aloof and lethargic. Though it was difficult to believe, the orcs – once held as the most aggressive race ever seen on Azeroth – had completely lost their will to fight. The strange lethargy confounded the Alliance leaders and continued to take its toll on the rapidly weakening orcs.

Some speculated that some strange disease, contractible only by orcs, brought about the baffling lethargy. But the Archmage, Antonidas of Dalaran, posed a different hypothesis. Researching what little he could find of orcish history, Antonidas learned that the orcs had been under the crippling influence of demonic power (or warlock magics) for generations. He speculated that the orcs had been corrupted by demonic powers even before their first invasion of Azeroth. Clearly, demons had spiked the orcs' blood, which in turn granted the brutes unnaturally heightened strength, endurance and aggression.

Antonidas theorized that the orcs' communal lethargy was not actually a disease, but a long-term racial withdrawal from the volatile Warlock magics that had made them fearsome, bloodlusted warriors. Though the symptoms were clear, Antonidas was unable to find a cure for the orcs' present condition. Many of his fellow mages, as well as a few notable Alliance leaders, argued that finding a cure for the orcs would be an imprudent venture. Left to ponder the orcs' mysterious condition, Antonidas' conclusion was that the orcs' only cure would have to be a spiritual one...

Thrall's Tale

During the dark days of the First War, a cunning human officer named Aedelas Blackmoore found an infant orc abandoned in the wilds. The infant orc, whom Blackmoore aptly named Thrall, was

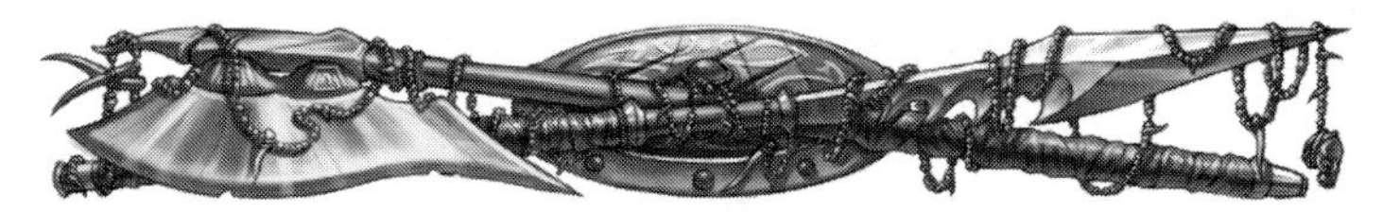

taken to the prison-fortress of Durnholde. There, Blackmoore raised the young orc as a favored slave and gladiator. Intending to train the young orc to be not only a peerless warrior, but also an educated leader, Blackmoore hoped to use Thrall to take over the horde, and thereby achieve dominion over his fellow men.

Nineteen years passed and Thrall grew into a strong, quick-witted orc. Yet his young heart knew that a slave's life was not for him. Many things had transpired in the world outside the fortress as he grew to maturity. He learned that his people, the orcs – whom he had never met – had been defeated and placed into internment camps in the human lands. Doomhammer, the leader of his people, had escaped from Lordaeron and gone into hiding. He knew that only one rogue clan still operated in secret, trying to evade the watchful eyes of the Alliance.

The resourceful yet inexperienced Thrall decided to escape from Blackmoore's fortress and set off to find others of his kind. During his journeys Thrall visited the internment camps and found his once mighty race to be strangely cowed and lethargic. Having not found the proud warriors he hoped to discover, Thrall set out to find the last undefeated orc chieftain, Grom Hellscream.

Despite being constantly hunted by the humans, Hellscream still held onto the horde's unquenchable will to fight. Aided only by his own devoted Warsong clan, Hellscream continued to fight an underground war against the oppression of his beleaguered people. Unfortunately, Hellscream could never find a way to rouse the captured orcs from their stupor. The impressionable Thrall, inspired by Hellscream's idealism, developed a strong empathy for the horde and its warrior traditions.

Seeking the truth of his own origins, Thrall traveled north to find the legendary Frostwolf clan. Thrall learned that Gul'dan had exiled the Frostwolves during the early days of the First War. He also discovered that he was the son and heir of the orc hero, Durotan – the true chieftain of the Frostwolves who had been murdered in the wilds nearly twenty years before...

Under the tutelage of the venerable shaman, Drek'Thar, Thrall studied the ancient shamanistic culture of his people that had been forgotten under Gul'dan's' evil rule. Over time, Thrall became a powerful shaman and took his rightful place as chieftain of the exiled Frostwolves. Empowered by the elements themselves and driven to find his destiny, Thrall set off to free the captive clans and heal his race of demonic corruption.

During his travels, Thrall found the aged warchief, Orgrim Doomhammer, who had been living as a hermit for many years. Doomhammer, who had been a close friend of Thrall's father, decided to follow the young, visionary orc and help him free the captive clans. Supported by many of the veteran chieftains, Thrall ultimately succeeded in revitalizing the horde and giving his people a new spiritual identity.

To symbolize his people's rebirth, Thrall returned to Blackmoore's fortress of Durnholde and put a decisive end to his former master's plans by laying siege to the internment camps. Yet, during the liberation of one camp, Doomhammer fell in battle. Thrall took up Doomhammer's legendary warhammer and donned his black plate-armor to become the new warchief of the horde. During the following months, Thrall's small but volatile horde laid waste to the internment camps and stymied the Alliance's best efforts to counter its clever strategies. Encouraged by his best friend and mentor, Grom Hellscream, Thrall worked to ensure that no orc would be cast into slavery – either by humans or demons – ever again.

Orc Hero Units

Blademaster

Though their numbers are few, the seasoned blademasters represent an elite fighting force within the horde. These skilled swordsmen were once part of the ill-fated Burning Blade clan that consumed itself in the throes of demonic corruption. With their clan scattered and broken, the proud blademasters swore a grim oath to free themselves and their brethren from demonic control once and for all. Under Thrall's command, the blademasters have once again joined the horde and serve as the young warchief's personal guard. Though blademasters are masters of stealth and guile, they value personal honor above all else.

BLADESTORM

By focusing their warrior energies, blademasters can become living cyclones of fighting rage. Spinning their great blades faster than the naked eye can see, they are capable of simultaneously damaging any enemy troops in their vicinity.

CRITICAL STRIKE

By channeling their potent powers in one focused strike, blademasters can cause even greater damage to their enemies.

MIRROR IMAGE

One of the blademasters' more mystical abilities is to create duplicate phantom images of themselves. Though the phantom images can move about freely of their own volition, they are not true entities unto themselves.

WIND WALK

So adept and agile are the blademasters that they can move so quickly that they appear to be invisible to the naked eye.

Far Seer

Far Seers are ancient orcs who represent the pinnacle of shamanistic power. These powerful shamans are counted amongst Thrall's closest advisors and are constantly in tune with the workings and maneuverings of the horde. Farseers are not only tied to the elements of the earth and sky, but are also adept at foretelling the future. Their wisdom is outshined only by their courage and ferocity in combat. When the enemies of the horde advance, the farseers mount their loyal dire wolves and wade into battle wielding all the elemental powers of their shamanistic birthright.

CHAIN LIGHTNING

Farseers have the ability to cast bolts of lightning so powerful that they continue to seek out enemy troops in a wide area of effect. The raging bolts continue to strike new victims until the spell's energies finally deplete.

EARTHQUAKE

Part of the Far Seers' power over nature is the ability to command the fury of the earth. When roused, farseers can cause the earth to quake violently. When called with precision, can cause heavy destruction to enemy structures and slow hapless foes.

FAR SIGHT

Far Seers have the uncanny ability to percieve distant places and events through a form of spirit sight. This ability allows them to anticipate enemy movements and maintain the element of surprise for the horde's fighting forces.

FERAL SPIRIT

One of the farseers' most otherworldy powers is their ability to call forth powerful wolven apparitions. As the Farseer gains experience, more powerful wolves may be summoned to his side.

Tauren Chieftain

These elder tauren warriors lead their tribes in daily life as well as in battle. Ceremoniously adorned with the ancient totems of their tribes, chieftains uphold the honor and simplicity of the proud tauren culture. When roused by battle, the gigantic chieftains employ enormous halberds that are capable of tearing through solid trees with one mighty swipe. The chieftains are fascinated by the orcs, especially their young leader, Thrall. They see an opportunity to help the orcs return to their traditional roots by providing a strong example of honor and courage through all tauren warriors.

ENDURANCE AURA

So heartening and stirring are the mighty chieftains that they exude an aura of strength and courage to all who accompany them. The chieftains' auras help their comrades to run and attack more quickly.

REINCARNATION

The tauren chieftains hold such sacred bonds with their Earthmother that they can actually be reincarnated after they die in combat. Though this ability is very rare, it makes the wise, benevolent chieftains a dangerous foe to threaten.

SHOCKWAVE

The mighty chieftains can swing their totems so hard that their impacts create powerful linear shockwaves that can damage any enemies bold enough to stand before them.

WAR STOMP

The tauren's massive totem can impact the ground with such force that every enemy within a wide radius of the chieftain is damaged and stunned for a short period of time.

Orc Units

Peon

The label of peon denotes the lowest station amongst those in the orcish horde. Inferior in all skills of import, these dredges are relegated to menial tasks such as harvesting lumber and mining gold. Their labor is also required for the construction and maintenance of buildings necessary to support the vast undertakings of the horde. Downtrodden, but exceedingly loyal, the orc peons toil endlessly to provide for the greater horde.

REPAIR

Peons can repair ruined or damaged orc structures through use of this valuable skill.

PILLAGE

Whenever Peons attack enemy structures, they can use this ability to gain resources to support more troops and build additional structures.

Grunt

Grunts are the first and last line of the horde's defense. These powerful fighters arm themselves with mighty battle-axes and display all of the savagery and cunning of their race. In past generations grunts were characterized by their depravity and brutality. But now, under the visionary leadership of Thrall, they more closely resemble their savage, yet noble warrior ancestors.

PILLAGE

Whenever Grunts attack enemy structures, they can use this ability to gain resources to support more troops and build additional structures.

Troll Headhunter

Though the horde allied itself with the evil forest trolls during the Second War, the alliance was short lived due to the horde's eventual defeat. But Thrall, on one of his many journeys, befriended a tribe of shadowy trolls from the steamy jungles of Stranglethorn

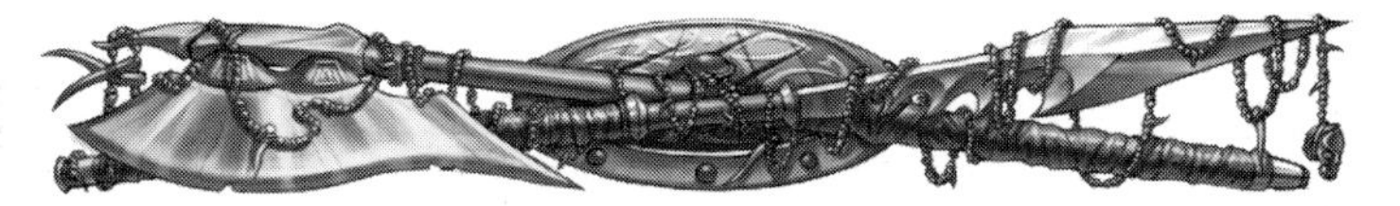

These cunning warriors are trained from birth to hunt, track and trap the most dangerous beasts in the wilds and possess the uncanny ability to regenerate lost health. In times of war, however, headhunters relish turning their mighty spears on the enemies of the horde without hesitation. Capable of hurling their deadly spears at distant enemies, troll headhunters provide invaluable cover fire for the other warriors of the horde.

TROLL REGENERATION

Like all trolls, headhunters can regenerate lost health over time. This racial ability makes the trolls fearsome opponents and often allows them to spring back into combat even though they've suffered grievous wounds.

Raider

The marauding, wolf-riding raiders were once considered to be the most honored warriors of the horde. Yet, just prior to the Second War, Gul'dan disbanded the raiders. Now, after many long years, the young warchief Thrall has decided to train a new generation of wolf riders. These mighty warriors carry hefty warblades into combat and rely greatly upon the cunning and ferocity of their faithful dire-wolf mounts to defeat their enemies.

ENSNARE

Raiders carry hand-sewn nets with which they can ensnare enemies. Though creatures will eventually break free from the nets, they are unable to move while caught. Flying creatures that are ensnared are brought to the ground.

PILLAGE

Whenever raiders attack enemy structures, they can they can use this ability to gain resources to support more troops and build additional structures.

Kodo Beast

The colossal kodo beasts of the Kalimdor plains are valued allies of the orcish horde. The mighty beasts were charged with carrying the orcs' pounding war drums into battle. The huge kodos, serving as symbols of orcish might and valor, also use their enormous size and strength to scatter enemy forces. When enraged, kodos are fond of devouring their enemies whole.

DEVOUR

Kodos are capable of swallowing enemy units whole. Enemy units can free their devoured comrades if they kill the kodo before the victim has been digested.

WAR DRUMS

The heartening rhythm of the orcish war drums drives the warriors of the horde to fight with greater strength and passion. Any allied warriors who hear the pounding drums gain bonuses to their already considerable fighting skills.

Shaman

Under the leadership of Thrall, the orcs have rediscovered their ancient shamanistic traditions. In an attempt to rid the horde of its demonic corruption, Thrall banned the use of warlock magic and necromancy. Now, all orc magic users practice shaman magic that draws its power from the natural world and the elements of the earth. Powerful shamans can call lightning from the sky and rouse the earth itself to devour legions of their enemies.

BLOODLUST

Shaman can cause such overwhelming bloodlust in their brethren that affected warriors actually increase in size and power for short periods of time.

LIGHTNING SHIELD

The shamans' lightning shields, when cast on fellow warriors, create a barrier that damages any nearby ground units.

PURGE

Shaman can purge any magical spells or enchantments from their comrades or enemies with their ability to purge. Though purge can be useful to remove negative enchantments or curses, it taxes the recipient to such a degree that the unit's movements are slow and painful.

Troll Witch Doctor

Although they are savage and cunning in the extreme, the troll witch doctors have aligned themselves with the horde out of pure necessity. These dastardly magic users are adept at manipulating the chemical processes within their fellow warriors in order to augment their combat abilities.

HEALING WARD

This strange tribal ward allows any friendly who comes in contact with it to heal their wounds and replenish their strength.

SENTRY WARD

Through this mysterious ward, witch doctors can keep watch over important areas for as long as the ward exists. Even though the wards will vanish in time, they are invaluable tools that enable the witch doctors to keep a constant eye on their surroundings.

STASIS TRAP

Only activated when enemy units cross its threshold, the stasis trap emits a strong shock of dark energy that immobilizes its victims and renders them helpless for a short duration of time.

Tauren

The mighty tauren of the Kalimdor plains have pledged their allegiance to the new horde out of respect for their courage and honor. The bold tauren seek only to safeguard their quiet culture from the deathly fires of the Burning Legion. When roused, tauren are fierce fighters and use their mighty totems to smash their enemies into the dust of the plains.

PULVERIZE

Tauren warriors can pulverize enemies by smashing their totems on the ground, creating tremendous shockwaves that ripple out and cause damage in a wide area of effect.

Catapult

The orcish catapult has always been a standing asset to the horde. Capable of hurling fiery projectiles over great distances, the catapults have been the doom of many Alliance regiments. Catapults serve as the horde's greatest siege weapon.

Wyvern Rider

The sentient wyverns of Kalimdor were eager to ally themselves with the shamanistic horde. Impressed by the orcs' commitment to honor and victory, the wyverns allowed the orcs to ride them into combat against those who would disturb the tranquility of Kalimdor and its denizens. The wyverns, who share a common ancestry with both dragons and gryphons, use their powerful claws and razor-like fangs against both airborne attackers and ground troops, while their riders may hurl envenomed spears at the enemy.

ENVENOMED WEAPONS

Wyvern riders carry envenomed spears that have been coated with the lethal venom from Stranglethorne's giant jungle snakes. When pierced by these spears, the riders' enemies are weakened and slowly eaten alive as the vile poison courses through their bodies.

Orc Structures

Great Hall

The great hall is the core stronghold of any orc clan. Using this structure, orcs process lumber and gold from mining operations are processed. Raw materials pilfered from enemy camps are added to the war chest. In time, the great hall can also be more heavily fortified.

Barracks

Barracks provide lodging for the orc troops. Sometimes a place of dissension within the lower ranks, the barracks houses not only orcs, but also bloodthirsty trolls. Here catapults are assembled and readied for war.

Burrow

These structures serve dual purposes: they act not only as farms for the harvesting of various roots and crops, but also as fortified bunkers for the peon workers to hide in during times of attack. Increasing numbers of these structures provide food to support the amassing of additional troops.

War Mill

An invention of the crafty trolls, this structure maximizes potential by serving as a mill for lumber as well as a forge for weapons smithing. Here weapons and armor are tirelessly reworked for maximum efficiency. Trolls here can also create one of their most useful fortifications: spiked barricades.

Stronghold

As clan technology advances, necessity dictates stronger fortifications and the ability to process the increasing income derived from pillaging enemy forces. This advancement enables the introduction of the shaman caste within the orc ranks. In time, the stronghold can be further modified to accommodate clan development.

Altar of Storms

Once used to channel the demonic energies of the Burning Legion, these altars have been retooled by troll masons. Using the rediscovered elemental abilities of the shamans, these altars serve as a kind of "gate" to revive fallen warriors. When a hero dies, his spirit can be recalled at these altars to continue service for the horde.

Beastiary

Using their kinship with the creatures of the wild, shamans and wyverns have struck a beneficial alliance. The deadly wyverns attack units both on land and in the air with equal efficiency. Raiders and giant kodo beasts, who have also been recruited into the ranks of the horde through shamanistic influence, are trained at this facility.

Spirit Lodge

The spirit lodge is a place of quiet contemplation where shamans and troll witch doctors meditate and refine their mastery of arcane magic. Having abandoned their practice of necromancy, magic users within the horde have found different ways to combat their enemies. Witch doctors manipulate chemicals within the body and in the environment, while shamans command the forces of nature.

Fortress

Once orc technology reaches its height, construction of the Fortress may begin. Far more formidable than even the stronghold, the fortress provides a siege-resistant command base. With the addition of spiked barricades, a Fortress may daunt even the most hostile foe.

Watch Tower

The horde's mighty watchtowers serve as the last line of defense for most orc towns. These sturdy structures were created to not

only stand guard over various orc holdings, but to detect and identify invisible or magically cloaked enemies as well.

Tauren Totem

The proud, noble tauren, having allied with the orcish horde, reside here and hone their abilities through contact with their spirit totems. This structure allows the mighty tauren to make use of the Pulverize ability, a technique that damages enemy forces and adds a unique tool to the tauren's already wide-ranging arsenal.

Undead Scourge
Undead History

The Shaman, Ner'zhul: Origin of the Lich King

The orcish clans, bound by a noble, shamanistic culture for thousands of years on the world of Draenor, knew nothing of corruption or spiritual decay. But the sinister agents of the Burning Legion sought to forge them into a voracious, unstoppable army. The cunning demon, Kil'jaeden, second in command of the Legion, saw that the savage warriors had vast potential for murder and bloodshed – and set out to corrupt their tranquil society from within.

Kil'jaeden appeared to the orcs' most respected leader, the elder shaman Ner'zhul, and told him that he would bestow upon the orcs great power and make them the undisputed rulers of their world. He even offered the old shaman untold mystical knowledge if he agreed to bind himself and his people to the Legion's will. Calculating and power hungry by nature, Ner'zhul accepted Kil'jaeden's offer and made a Blood Pact with the demon. By doing so, Ner'zhul had sealed the orcs' fate and damned them to become the unwitting slaves of the Burning Legion.

As time passed, Kil'jaeden recognized that Ner'zhul did not have the will or the brazen audacity to follow through with his plan of forging the orcs into a bloodthirsty horde. Ner'zhul, realizing that his pact with Kil'jaeden would only lead to his race's annihilation, refused to help the demon any further. Enraged by the shaman's defiance, Kil'jaeden swore to take vengeance upon Ner'zhul, and corrupt the orcs despite him. Kil'jaeden found a new, eager apprentice to lead the orcs on the path to oblivion - Ner'zhul's own nefarious protégé, Gul'dan.

With Kil'jaeden's help, Gul'dan succeeded where his teacher had faltered. The evil, power-hungry orc not only abolished the ancient practice of shamanism – which he replaced with the study of demonic warlock magics – but united the orc clans into the volatile horde that Kil'jaeden had envisioned. Ner'zhul, powerless to stop his former apprentice, could only watch as Gul'dan masterfully transformed the orcs into mindless agents of destruction.

Years passed as Ner'zhul brooded silently upon the red world of Draenor. He watched as his people staged the first invasion of Azeroth. He heard the tales of the orcs' Second War against the Alliance of Lordaeron. He bore witness to the treachery and corruption that seemed to be destroying his people from within. Despite Gul'dan's masterminding the horde's dark destiny,

Ner'zhul knew that he himself was responsible for setting it all in motion.

Shortly after the end of the Second War, the news of the horde's defeat reached the orcs who had remained in Draenor. Ner'zhul, knowing that the horde had failed its mission to conquer Azeroth, feared that Kil'jaeden and the Legion would take dire action against the remaining orcs. To escape Kil'jaeden's imminent wrath, Ner'zhul opened a number of mystical portals that lead to new, unspoiled worlds. The old shaman rallied the remaining orc clans and planned to lead them through one of the portals, and into a new directed destiny.

Before he could execute his plan, Ner'zhul was forced to deal with an Alliance expeditionary force sent to Draenor to destroy the orcs forever. Ner'zhul's loyal clans managed to hold the Alliance forces at bay while the old shaman opened the raging, magical portals. To his horror, Ner'zhul realized that the portals' tremendous energies were beginning to rip the very fabric of Draenor apart. As the Alliance forces pushed the orcs further back into the hellish world, Draenor began to buckle in on itself. Realizing that the battling clans would never reach the portals in time, Ner'zhul selfishly abandoned them and escaped with his elite followers in tow. The evil group of orcs crossed through their chosen portal just as Draenor blew apart in an apocalyptic explosion. The old shaman believed he'd been lucky to escape death… Ironically, he would live to regret his náiveté.

Kil'jaeden and the New Deal

Just as Ner'zhul and his followers entered the Twisting Nether – the ethereal plane that connects all of the worlds scattered throughout the Great Dark Beyond – they were ambushed by Kil'jaeden and his demonic minions. Kil'jaeden, who had sworn to take vengeance on Ner'zhul for his prideful defiance, tortured the old shaman mercilessly by slowly tearing his body apart piece by piece. Kil'jaeden kept the shaman's spirit alive and intact – leaving Ner'zhul painfully aware of his body's gross dismemberment. Though Ner'zhul pleaded with the demon to release his spirit and grant him death, the demon grimly replied that the Blood Pact they had made long ago was still binding – and that he would make use of his wayward pawn once again.

The orcs' failure to conquer Azeroth as the Legion intended, forced Kil'jaeden to create a new army to sew chaos throughout the kingdoms of the Alliance. This new army could not be allowed to fall prey to the same petty rivalries and infighting that had plagued the horde. It would have to be dogged, merciless, and single-minded in its mission. This time, Kil'jaeden could not afford to fail.

Holding Ner'zhul's tortured, helpless spirit in stasis, Kil'jaeden gave him one last chance to serve the Legion or suffer eternal torment. Once again, Ner'zhul recklessly agreed to the demon's pact.

Ner'zhul's spirit was placed within a specially crafted block of diamond-hard ice gathered from the far reaches of the Twisting Nether. Encased within the frozen cask, Ner'zhul felt his consciousness expand ten thousand fold. Warped by the demon's chaotic powers, Ner'zhul became a spectral being of unfathomable power. At that moment, the orc known as Ner'zhul was shattered forever, and the Lich King was born.

Ner'zhul's loyal death knights and warlock followers were also transformed by the demon's chaotic energies. The wicked spell casters were ripped apart and remade as skeletal Liches. The demons had ensured that even in death, Ner'zhul's followers would serve him unquestioningly.

When the time was right, Kil'jaeden patiently explained the mission for which he had created the Lich King: Ner'zhul was to spread a plague of death and terror across Azeroth that would snuff out human civilization forever. All those who died from the dreaded plague would arise as the undead... and their spirits would be bound to Ner'zhul's iron will forever. Kil'jaeden promised that if Ner'zhul accomplished his dark mission of scouring humanity from the world, he would be freed from his curse and granted a new, healthy body to inhabit.

Though Ner'zhul was agreeable and seemingly anxious to play his part, Kil'jaeden remained skeptical of his pawn's loyalties. Keeping the Lich King bodiless and trapped within the crystal cask assured his good conduct for the short term, but the demon knew that he would need to keep a watchful eye on the Lich King. To this end, Kil'jaeden called upon his elite demon guard, the vampiric Dreadlords, to police Ner'zhul and ensure that he accomplished his dread task. Tichondrius, the most powerful and cunning of the Dreadlords, warmed to the challenge, fascinated by the plague's severity and the Lich King's unbridled potential for genocide.

Icecrown and the Frozen Throne

Kil'jaeden cast Ner'zhul's icy cask back into the world of Azeroth. The hardened crystal streaked across the night sky and smashed into the desolate, arctic continent of Northrend, burying itself in the deep, shadowed hallows of the Icecrown glacier. The frozen crystal, warped and scarred by its violent descent, came to resemble a throne, and Ner'zhul's vengeful spirit stirred within it.

From the confines of the Frozen Throne, Ner'zhul began to reach out his vast consciousness and touch the minds of Northrend's native inhabitants. With surprising ease, he enslaved the minds of many indigenous creatures, such as ice trolls and the fierce wendigo - and drew their evil brethren into his growing shadow. He found that his psychic powers were almost limitless, and used them to create a small army that he housed within Icecrown's twisting labyrinths. As the Lich King mastered his growing powers under the Dreadlords' persistent vigil, he discovered a remote human settlement on the fringe of the vast Dragonblight. Ner'zhul decided to test his powers and his dread plague on the unsuspecting humans.

Ner'zhul sent the plague of undeath, which had originated from deep within the Frozen Throne, out into the arctic wasteland. Controlling the plague with his will alone, he drove it straight into the human village. Within three days, every human soul in the settlement was dead. Yet, in a surprisingly short amount of time, the dead villagers began to rise as zombified corpses. Ner'zhul could feel their individual spirits and thoughts as if they were his own. The raging cacophony in his mind caused Ner'zhul to grow even more powerful – as if their spirits provided him with much needed nourishment. He found it was child's play to control the zombies' actions and steer them to whatever end he wished.

Over the following months, Ner'zhul continued to experiment with his plague of undeath by subjugating every human inhabitant of Northrend. With his army of undead growing daily, he knew that the time for his true test was nearing.

War of the Spider

For ten long years, Ner'zhul built up his power base in Northrend. A great citadel was erected above Icecrown and manned by growing legions of the undead. Yet, as the Lich King extended his influence over the land, a lone, shadowy empire stood against his power. The ancient, subterranean kingdom of Azjol-Nerub, which had been founded by a race of sinister humanoid spiders, sent their elite warrior-guard to attack Icecrown and end the Lich King's mad bid for dominance. Much to his frustration, Ner'zhul found that the evil Nerubians were immune to not only the plague, but to his telepathic domination as well.

The Nerubian spider lords commanded vast forces and had an underground network that stretched nearly half the breadth of Northrend. Their hit and run tactics on the Lich King's strongholds stymied his efforts to root them out time after time. Ultimately, Ner'zhul's war against the Nerubians was won by attrition. With the aid of the furious Dreadlords and his innumerable undead warriors, the Lich King invaded Azjol-Nerub and brought its subterranean temples crashing down upon the spider lords' heads.

Though the Nerubians were immune to his plague, Ner'zhul's growing necromantic powers allowed him to raise the spider warriors' corpses and bend them to his will. As a testament to their tenacity and fearlessness, Ner'zhul adopted the Nerubians' distinctive architectural style for his own fortresses and structures. Left to rule his kingdom unopposed, the Lich King began preparing for his true mission in the world. Reaching out into the human lands with his vast consciousness, the Lich King called out to any dark soul that would listen...

Kel'Thuzad and the Cult of the Damned

There were a handful of powerful individuals, scattered across the world, who heard the Lich King's mental summons. Most notable of them was the Archmage, Kel'Thuzad, of the magical nation of Dalaran. Kel'Thuzad, one of senior members of the Kirin Tor – Dalaran's ruling council – had been considered a maverick for years due to his insistence on studying the forbidden arts of necromancy. Driven to learn all he could of the magical world and its shadowy wonders, he was frustrated by what he saw as his peers' outmoded and unimaginative precepts. Upon hearing the powerful summons from Northrend, the Archmage bent all of his considerable will to communing with the mysterious voice. Convinced that the Kirin Tor was too squeamish to seize the power and knowledge inherent in the dark arts, he vowed to learn what he could from the immensely powerful Lich King.

Forsaking his fortune and prestigious political standing, Kel'Thuzad abandoned the ways of the Kirin Tor and left Dalaran forever. Prodded by the Lich King's persistent voice in his mind, he sold his vast holdings and stored away his fortunes. Travelling alone over many leagues of both land and sea, he finally reached the frozen shores of Northrend. Intent on reaching Icecrown and offering his services to the Lich King, the Archmage passed through the ravaged, war-torn ruins of Azjol-Nerub. Kel'Thuzad saw firsthand the scope and ferocity of Ner'zhul's power. He began to believe that allying himself with the mysterious Lich King would not only be wise, but potentially fruitful.

After long months of trekking through the harsh arctic wastelands, Kel'Thuzad finally reached the dark glacier of Icecrown. He boldly approached Ner'zhul's dark citadel and was shocked when the silent undead guardsmen let him pass as though he was expected. Kel'Thuzad descended deep into the cold earth and found his way down to the bottom of the glacier. There, in the endless cavern of ice and shadows, he prostrated himself before the Frozen Throne and offered his soul to the dark lord of the dead.

The Lich King was pleased with his latest conscript. He promised Kel'Thuzad immortality and great power in exchange for his loyalty and obedience. Kel'Thuzad, eager for dark knowledge and power, accepted his first great mission – to go into the world of men and found a new religion that would worship the Lich King as a god.

To help the Archmage accomplish his mission, Ner'zhul left Kel'Thuzad's humanity intact. The aged, yet still charismatic wizard was charged with using his powers of illusion and persuasion to lull the downtrodden, disenfranchised masses of Lordaeron into a confidence. Once he had their attention, he would offer them a new vision of what society could be – and a new figurehead to call their king... .

Kel'Thuzad returned to Lordaeron in disguise, and over the span of three years, he used his fortune and intellect to gather a clandestine brotherhood of like-minded men and women. The brotherhood, which he called the Cult of the Damned, promised its acolytes social equality and eternal life on Azeroth in exchange for their service and obedience to Ner'zhul. As the months passed, Kel'Thuzad found many eager volunteers for his new cult amongst the tired, overburdened laborers of Lordaeron. Surprisingly, Kel'Thuzad's goal to pervert the citizens' faith in the Holy Light towards belief in Ner'zhul's dark shadow was easily attained. As the Cult of the Damned grew in size and influence, Kel'Thuzad made sure to keep its workings secret from the authorities of Lordaeron at every turn.

The Forming of the Scourge

With Kel'Thuzad's success in Lordaeron, the Lich King made the final preparations for his assault against human civilization. Placing his plague energies into a number of portable artifacts called plague cauldrons, Ner'zhul ordered Kel'Thuzad to transport the cauldrons to Lordaeron where they would be hidden within various cult-controlled villages. The cauldrons, protected by the loyal cultists, would then act as plague generators, sending the plague seeping out across the unsuspecting farmlands and cities of northern Lordaeron.

The Lich King's plan worked perfectly. Many of Lordaeron's northern villages were contaminated almost immediately. Just as in Northrend, the citizens who contracted the plague died and arose as the Lich King's willing slaves. The cultists under Kel'Thuzad were eager to die and be raised again in their dark lord's service. They exulted in the prospect of immortality through undeath. As the plague spread, more and more feral zombies arose in the northlands. Kel'Thuzad looked upon the Lich King's growing army and named it the Scourge – for soon, it would march upon the gates of Lordaeron...and scour humanity from the face of the world.

An Heir Apparent...

Though the Dreadlords were pleased that Ner'zhul's true mission had finally begun, the Lich King himself brooded within the tight, shadowy confines of the Frozen Throne. Despite his vast psychic powers and his complete dominion over the undead, he longed to be free of his icy prison. He knew that Kil'jaeden would never release him from his curse. And, due to his great power, he knew that the demons would destroy him as soon as his mission was completed.

Still, he had one chance for freedom – one chance to escape his terrible curse. If he could find a suitable host – some hapless dupe who was torn between darkness and light – he could possess that body and escape the confines of the Frozen Throne forever.

Thus, the Lich King sent his vast consciousness out once again and sought out the perfect host...

Undead Hero Units

Lich

While on Draenor, Ner'zhul commanded a number of orcish warlocks and spell-wielding death knights. Yet, when Kil'jaeden and the Legion captured these sorcerers after that world's destruction, they were transformed into twisted, spectral aberrations of their former selves. These newly born liches possessed tremendous magical powers, yet their immortal, undead bodies were bound to the iron will of Ner'zhul. As payment for their undying loyalty to Ner'zhul, the Lich King granted them control over the furious elements of Northrend. Now, the liches wield frost magic along with their own considerable necromantic spells.

FROST NOVA

Liches can call upon the freezing energies of Northrend to do their bidding. Using a single enemy as the focal point for their dire spell, liches can cause an explosion of frost to burst from the targeted creature that will damage everything around it. Creatures harmed in this way have trouble moving, incapacitated by the freezing ice that stiffens their joints.

FROST ARMOR

An allied creature can be encased in a protective armor of ice. Creatures attacking the Frost Armor have difficulty moving due to the jolt of freezing cold that moves through their bodies.

DARK RITUAL

By destroying one of his own minions, the Lich is able to absorb the energies of his lesser comrade, replenishing his dark magical powers. The lich can absorb the energies of his undead army by casting a Dark Ritual on them. Though this destroys the lich's lesser comrades, it releases their energies back into the lich and replenishes the Lich's power.

DEATH AND DECAY

The swirling negative energies known as the Death And Decay spell are favored by the liches for their power to decompose, rot and destroy everything within them. Not even the strongest warriors or the most durable structures can stand the full effects of Death And Decay.

Death Knight

Death knights were once heroic, virtuous defenders of humanity. However, they were corrupted by the subtle machinations of the Lich King and lured to his dark standard. These former heroes were given untold power and the promise of immortality in exchange for their loyalties. Although they retained their humanity, their twisted souls were bound to the Lich King's will for all time. Bestowed with black, vampiric runeblades and shadowy steeds, death knights now serve as the Scourge's mightiest generals.

DEATH COIL

Death knights can call upon the forces of darkness at will, causing bolts of death to issue from their hands. While doing considerable damage to the death knights' enemies, the Death Coil also heals their undead brethren.

DEATH PACT

Through the sacrifice of his followers, a death knight can absorb their unholy energies and convert them into health for himself.

ANIMATE DEAD

Arguably the death knights' most horrific power is their ability to raise recently slain corpses into an army of the undead, no matter what their allegiance in life may have been. Though they are brought back for a time, the death knights' recalled warriors will eventually fall, never to be raised again.

UNHOLY AURA

All death knights can learn to exude a dark, raging battle aura that causes allied creatures around them to move and regenerate life more quickly.

Dreadlord

Dreadlords are incredibly powerful demons who wield the powers of darkness and mental domination. These cunning, malefic beings once served as the demon Kil'jaeden's most trusted lieutenants. Yet, at Kil'jaeden's request, the vampiric Dreadlords were sent to watch over the Lich King, Ner'zhul, and ensure that he carried out his orders to sow chaos in the mortal world. Though Dreadlords have been known to revel in the gore of single combat, they generally prefer to manipulate and beguile their enemies from the shadows.

CARRION SWARM

Dreadlords control the creatures of the night, and some of them have even mastered the ability to call swarms of bats and insects to strike at their unsuspecting enemies.

SLEEP
Through the mastery of subversion and hypnosis, Dreadlords have learned to put their enemies into a sudden, trance-like sleep. Though this mystical sleep will wear off in time, a sharp jab from either a friend or an enemy will always awaken the hapless sleeper.

VAMPIRIC AURA
Those who are fortunate enough to have a powerful Dreadlord as an ally can gain the benefits of his Vampiric Aura. This dark, unholy aura causes the Dreadlord's allies to actually gain life by spilling their enemies' blood.

INFERNO
The Dreadlord marks the pinnacle of his dark powers with the devastating ability to summon a fiery infernal. At his call, the infernal will streak down from the sky, stunning and wounding nearby enemy forces when it crashes to the earth. The infernal, engulfed in searing flame, will then rise to do the dreadlord's bidding.

UNDEAD UNITS

Acolyte
Acolytes are human beings who have given themselves over to the power of Ner'zhul and the Scourge. These bitter, fanatical men and women will stop at nothing to promote the Lich King's will and maintain the secrecy and dominance of the Cult of the Damned. They view their own deaths and the possibility of becoming undead as the ultimate rewards for the service to Ner'zhul.

UNSUMMON
The unsummoning of buildings allows the acolytes of the Scourge to reduce fully constructed buildings to their base forms of matter and energy. Some of this matter and energy is lost in the conversion, as are most things that are pulled through The Great Dark Beyond.

SACRIFICE
Acolytes who wish to serve as the eyes and ears of Ner'zhul are capable of shedding their bodies and taking on the forms of invisible Shades.

Ghoul
Ghouls are the basic warriors of the undead Scourge. These lumbering, rotting corpses were once innocent townsfolk who have made the final transition into true undeath. Ghouls have great stamina and revel in combat with living beings. Ghouls are ravenous cannibals who can regenerate their health by eating the flesh of fallen warriors.

CANNIBALIZE
Ghouls that are wounded can consume the flesh of the newly dead to replenish their own lost health.

Necromancer

Though they retained their humanity after making their pact with death, necromancers became some of the most terrifying agents of the Scourge. These dark, nefarious men were once thought to be aspiring geniuses by the Magocracy of Dalaran. However, their insatiable lust to delve into the dark arts drove them to forsake their very souls. Ner'zhul, the Lich King, granted these malevolent sorcerers true power over the dead in exchange for their obedience. The shadowy necromancers have the power to raise skeletal warriors from the grave and bestow a number of dark enchantments upon their fellow warriors.

RAISE DEAD

Through the powers of Ner'zhul, the corpses of the recently slain can be raised again as skeleton warriors. Though relentless and fearless, these mindless automatons of death soon fall apart and fall to dust.

UNHOLY FRENZY

With their unholy powers, necromancers can greatly accelerate a creature's movement and attack rates. Those under the influence of this spell find themselves moving so quickly that their bodies begin to burn and ache, slowly dying from the effects of their unholy frenzy.

CRIPPLE

Drawing dark energies directly from Ner'zhul, necromancers can cause their enemies' muscles to suddenly spasm and quake – leaving them immobile and effectively helpless.

Abomination

The twisted, mutilated bodies of the abominations are comprised of multiple dead limbs and body parts from many different corpses. These enormous warriors, scarred by loose stitchings and putrid, open sores, love to carve flesh and tear their enemies apart. The slow-moving and dull-witted abominations constantly drip blood and smell like disease-ridden slaughterhouses. They carry large cleavers into combat and wield various sickle-bladed hooks on their disproportionate limbs.

DISEASE CLOUD

A cloud of festering rotten flesh-vapors follows the abominations wherever they go. The vile cloud is renowned for rotting living flesh upon contact. This nameless disease is often spread to meat wagons, thus allowing the contraptions' rotting ammunition to deal further damage to the enemies of the Scourge.

Banshee

Banshees were once beautiful female elves who fell before the power of the Scourge. Their restless spirits were left to wander the world in silent, tortured lamentation. Then, the Lich King gathered them together and gave them terrible voices so that the living would finally

hear their bitter anguish. Thus, the banshees have pledged themselves to Ner'zhul's cause and now serve as valuable agents of the Scourge. On certain nights, when the moon is full, their unnerving, unholy screams can be heard in the icy winds blowing from the north.

CURSE

By channeling the powers of their unholy screams, banshees can cause their enemies to temporarily lose their honed combat skills. As a result of this terrible curse, the victims of this spell find themselves unable to hit their targets.

ANTI-MAGIC SHELL

By melding the powers of necromancy and the warped music of their screams, banshees can form protective shells around any creatures. The uncanny "shell" makes those creatures impervious to all magics for a short period of time.

POSSESSION

Banshees have an unsettling ability to force their way into the bodies of living creatures, thus replacing the creatures' spirits with their own. While this ability causes the banshees' bodies to dissipate, it does give them permanent control over their new forms.

Gargoyles

The dreaded gargoyles of Northrend are voracious flying creatures who revel in slaughter and mayhem. Brought from the frozen north by the armies of the Lich King, these strange, wiry flyers have rough, crystalline hides which protect them from all manner of attacks. In times of great peril, gargoyles can land and condense their hides into a stone-like surface. Though they are unable to attack in this state, they can take time to regenerate their wounds and replenish their energies.

STONE FORM

The voracious gargoyles of Northrend are capable of condensing their crystalline hides to make themselves nearly impervious to any forms of attacks. Though they must land and remain motionless while in this state, Stone Form does allow them to recoup their energies for battle.

Crypt Fiend

The cunning crypt fiends were once the lords of the ancient spider kingdom of Azjol-Nerub that ruled over the arctic land of Northrend in ancient times. However, the Lich King destroyed the crypt fiends' civilization and took control of the frozen continent. Now the vile fiends command their spider underlings in the name of their master, Ner'zhul. These aberrant creatures are capable of summoning swarms of vile insects and projecting web-like strands to incapacitate and harm their enemies.

WEB

The crypt fiends of Azjol-Nerub have always been adept at catching flying creatures in their powerful webbing. Though creatures captured in this webbing will eventually break free and may still defend themselves, they are immobilized while caught in the crypt fiends' webs.

Frost Wyrm

In ages past, venerable dragons nearing death flew to the land of Northrend to die. To this day there are entire dragon graveyards littered with massive petrified bones and skulls. When Ner'zhul, the Lich King, took control of Northrend, he used his powerful magics to raise the ancient dragon skeletons from the dead. Now the skeletal dragons radiate cold power and think of nothing other than serving their dark master. Frost wyrms have a cold-based breath weapon that can shatter entire buildings. They are also quite fond of devouring their hapless enemies whole.

FREEZING BREATH

Ner'zhul's vicious frost wyrms hold the frosts of Northrend within their skeletal hearts. By inhaling a great deal of air, frost wyrms can expel blasts of freezing cold so extreme, that they pull all the moisture from the air around a building and freezes it solid.

Meat Wagon

One of the strangest and most dire tools utilized by the Scourge is the dreaded meat wagon. This rickety contraption is used to collect and store recently slain corpses from the field of battle. At any time, corpses can be pulled from the meat wagon and raised into undead warriors. When upgraded, the Meat Wagon can also fling diseased corpses at enemy units with its crude catapult device. An invaluable support vehicle for the Scourge, the meat wagon strikes fear and woe into the hearts of even the most resolute defenders.

Skeletal Warrior

Called forth from the grave by the insidious necromancers, skeletal warriors are mindless slaves of the Lich King's powers. These lumbering fighters are highly resilient and tireless. When operating in great numbers, skeleton warriors serve as an invaluable part of the Scourge's combat force.

Shade

Called forth from the depths of the sacrificial pits, shades are vile, wraith-like creatures who exist only to serve their dark lord, Ner'zhul. The invisible shades are virtually undetectable by normal sight, making them ideal scouts and spies for the Scourge. Though they cannot attack the living, they are still considered valuable assets to the Lich King's forces.

Undead Structures

Necropolis

The necropolis serves as the central command structure of the undead army. Lumber harvested by ghouls is processed and loyal acolytes train for tasks from their undead masters. Even when unattended, the vengeful spirits of the dead protect the necropolis from enemy attackers. In time this structure can be further modified to become the halls of the dead.

Crypt

At this site, undead minions are summoned into the service of the Scourge. Here gargoyles are made animate and given deadly attack capabilities. Ghouls are trained to cannibalizing fallen foes to renew strength. Crypt fiends are empowered to cast their inescapable webs.

Graveyard

Servants of the Undead tirelessly study the arcane arts in an effort to imbue weapons and armor with unholy power. The graveyard, like the necropolis, is able to process lumber for weapon and armor construction. This building also pulls fresh corpses from deep within the earth, exhuming them for use by the vile necromancers.

Ziggurat

These towers of the ancient spider kingdom of Azjol-Nerub are called into service once again to provide a source of raw energy for undead forces. Several ziggurats are required to sustain a high number of Scourge warriors. In time, these towers can be further empowered to provide protection.

Spirit Tower

Once infused with the restless spirits of the vengeful dead, spirit towers present a formidable defense. The wraiths of the tower attack with supernatural efficiency, and quickly add enemy forces to the ranks of dead. Multiple towers in an undead city will chill the heart of even the most courageous foe.

Halls of the Dead

As the presence of the Undead in the living world grows stronger, further modifications to the command structure become necessary. Transforming a necropolis into the halls of the dead gives the Scourge power to raise more ancient structures and advance their cruel efficiency. With continued advancement, the halls of the dead may be further modified.

Temple of the Damned

Once used by the orcish horde to channel demonic energies, the Scourge has now reclaimed this powerful edifice. From the Temple the insidious necromancers emerge to animate fallen corpses and the tormented spirits of the banshees are called into service.

Slaughterhouse

Meat at the slaughterhouse is used to serve the twisted purpose of the malevolent Scourge. Grotesque, monstrous abominations are pieced together and instilled with the single purpose of killing. Meat wagons are constructed to lob plague-infected body parts at the enemy.

Altar of Darkness

This structure serves as a channeling nexus for the Scourge's dark restorative powers. When a hero falls in battle, his essence may be recalled to this site, where it is given new, unholy life. Provided that the building stands and resources are sufficient, undead heroes will not stay dead for long.

Black Citadel

When the powers of the Undead in the living world become fully manifested, further modifications to the halls of the dead become necessary. Building of the black citadel allows the Scourge to operate at peak efficiency. Along with this modification comes increased fortification, making the black citadel a truly formidable stronghold.

Boneyard

The boneyard is the home of the frost wyrms, once magnificent dragons now reduced to skeletal frames, manipulated by the dark magic of the Scourge to serve the Lich King. Frost wyrms have a crippling ability to cast their freezing breath onto enemy forces and buildings. In large numbers, frost wyrms present a truly dominating force.

Sacrificial Pit

The sacrificial pits of Azjol-Nerub were used long ago to sacrifice enemy forces in exchange for success in battle. Undead forces may be sacrificed at this location to call forth a shade, an invisible wraith capable of spying on the enemy, detectable only through magic.

Night Elves: the Sentinels

Night Elf History

The Kaldorei and the Well of Eternity

Ten thousand years before the orcs and humans clashed in their First War, the world of Azeroth cradled only one massive continent surrounded by the infinite, raging seas. That land mass, known as Kalimdor, was home to a number of disparate races and creatures, all vying for survival amongst the savage elements of the waking world. At the dark continent's center was a mysterious lake of incandescent energies. The lake, which would later be called the Well of Eternity, was the true heart of the world's magic and natural power. Drawing its energies from the infinite Great Dark beyond the world, the Well acted as a mystical fount, sending its potent energies out across the world to nourish life in all its wondrous forms.

In time, a primitive tribe of nocturnal humanoids cautiously made their way to the edges of the mesmerizing, enchanted lake. The feral, nomadic humanoids, drawn by the Well's strange energies, built crude homes upon its tranquil shores. Over time, the Well's cosmic power affected the strange tribe, making them strong, wise and virtually immortal. The tribe adopted the name Kaldorei, which meant "children of the stars" in their native tongue. To celebrate their budding society, they constructed great structures and temples around the lake's periphery.

The Kaldorei, or night elves as they would later be known, worshipped the moon goddess, Elune, and believed that she slept within the Well's shimmering depths during the daylight hours. The early night elf priests and seers studied the Well with an insatiable curiosity, driven to plumb its untold secrets and power. As their society grew, the night elves explored the breadth of Kalimdor and encountered its myriad denizens. The only creatures that gave them pause were the ancient and powerful dragons. Though the great serpentine beasts were often reclusive, they did much to safeguard the known lands from potential threats. The night elves believed that the dragons held themselves to be the protectors of the world, and that they and their secrets were best left alone.

In time, the night elves' curiosity led them to meet and befriend a number of powerful entities, not the least of which was Cenarius, a mighty demi-god of the primordial forestlands. The great-hearted Cenarius grew fond of the inquisitive night elves and spent a great deal of time teaching them about the natural world. The tranquil Kaldorei developed a strong empathy for the living forests of Kalimdor and reveled in the harmonious balance of nature.

Yet, as the seemingly endless ages passed, the night elves' civilization expanded both territorially and culturally. Their temples, roads, and dwelling places stretched across the breadth of the dark continent. Azshara, the night elves' beautiful and gifted Queen, built an immense, wondrous palace on the Well's shore that housed her favored servitors within its bejeweled halls. Her servitors, whom she called the Quel'dorei or "high-borne," doted on her every command and believed themselves to be greater than the rest of their lower-caste brethren. Though Queen Azshara was loved equally by all of her people, the high-borne were secretly hated by the jealous masses.

Sharing the priests' curiosity towards the Well of Eternity, Azshara ordered the educated high-borne to plumb its secrets and reveal its true purpose in the world. The high-borne buried themselves in their work and studied the Well ceaselessly. In time they developed the ability to manipulate and control the Well's cosmic energies. As their reckless experiments progressed, the high-borne found that they could use their newfound powers to either create or destroy at their leisure. The hapless high-borne had stumbled upon primitive magic and were now resolved to devote themselves to its mastery. Although they agreed that magic was inherently dangerous if handled irresponsibly, Azshara and her high-borne began to practice their spellcraft with reckless abandon. Cenarius and many of the wizened night elf scholars warned that only calamity would result from toying with the clearly volatile arts of magic. But, Azshara and her followers stubbornly continued to expand their burgeoning powers.

As their powers grew, a distinct change came over Azshara and the high-borne. The haughty, aloof upper class became increasingly callous and cruel towards their fellow night elves. A dark, brooding pall veiled Azshara's once entrancing beauty. She began to withdraw from her loving subjects and refused to interact with any but her trusted high-borne priests.

A young, brazen scholar named Furion Stormrage, who had spent much of his time studying the Well's effects, began to suspect that a terrible power was corrupting the high-borne and his beloved Queen. Though he could not conceive the evil that was to come, he knew that the night elves' lives would soon be changed forever...

The War of the Ancients

The high-borne's reckless use of magic sent ripples of energy spiraling out from the Well of Eternity and into the Great Dark Beyond. The ripples of energy streamed out into the Twisting Nether and were felt by terrible alien minds. Sargeras, the Great Enemy of all life, the Ravager of Worlds, felt the potent ripples and was drawn to their distant point of origin. Spying the primordial world of Azeroth and sensing the limitless energies of the Well of Eternity, Sargeras was consumed by an insatiable hunger. The great, dark god of the Nameless Void resolved to destroy the fledgling world and claim its energies as his own.

Sargeras gathered his vast, demonic army, known as the Burning Legion, and made his way towards the unsuspecting world of Azeroth. The Legion, comprised of a million screaming demons, all ripped from the far corners of the universe, roiled and burned at the thought of conquest. Sargeras' lieutenants, Archimonde the Defiler and Mannoroth the Destructor, prepared their infernal minions to strike.

Queen Azshara, overwhelmed by the terrible ecstasy of her magic, fell victim to Sargeras' undeniable power, and agreed to grant him entrance to her world. Even her high-borne servitors gave themselves over to magic's inevitable corruption and began to worship Sargeras as their god. To show their allegiance to the Legion, the high-borne aided their Queen in opening a great, swirling portal within the depths of the Well of Eternity.

Once all his preparations had been made, Sargeras began his catastrophic invasion of Azeroth. The warrior-demons of the Burning Legion stormed into the world through the Well of Eternity and laid siege to the night elves' sleeping cities. Led by Archimonde and Mannoroth, the Legion swarmed over the lands of Kalimdor leaving only ash and sorrow in its wake. The demon warlocks called down the searing Infernals that crashed, like hellish meteors, into the graceful spires of Kalimdor's temples. The Doomguard, a band of burning, bloodletting killers, marched across Kalimdor's fields slaughtering everyone in their path. Even packs of wild, demonic Felhounds ravaged the countryside, unopposed. Though the brave Kaldorei warriors rushed to defend their ancient homeland, they were forced to give ground, inch by inch, before the fury of the Legion's onslaught.

The Sundering of the World

It fell to the young scholar, Furion Stormrage, to find help for his beleaguered people. Stormrage, whose own brother, Illidan, practiced the high-borne's magics, was incensed by the growing corruption amongst the upper class. Convincing Illidan to forsake his dangerous obsession, Furion set out to find Cenarius and muster a resistance force. The young, beautiful priestess, Tyrande, agreed to accompany the brothers in the name of Elune. Though both Furion and Illidan shared a secret love for the idealistic priestess, Tyrande's heart belonged to Furion alone. Illidan resented his brother's budding romance with Tyrande, but knew that his heartache was nothing compared to the pain of his magical addiction...

Illidan, who had grown dependent on magic's empowering energies, struggled to keep control of himself and his overwhelming hunger to tap the Well's energies once again. However, with Tyrande's patient support, he was able to contain himself and help his brother find the reclusive demi-god, Cenarius. Cenarius, who dwelt within the sacred Moonglades of the distant Mount Hyjal, agreed to help the night elves by finding the ancient dragons and enlisting their aid. The dragons, led by the great, red leviathan, Alexstrasza, agreed to send their mighty flights to engage the demons and their infernal masters.

Cenarius, calling on the spirits of the enchanted forests, rallied an army of ancient tree-men and led them against the Legion in a daring ground assault. As the night elves' allies converged upon Azshara's temple and the Well of Eternity, all-out warfare erupted. Despite the strength of their newfound allies, Furion and his colleagues realized that the Legion could not be defeated by martial strength alone.

As the titanic battle raged around Azshara's capital city, the delusional Queen waited in anticipation for Sargeras' arrival. The Lord of the Legion was preparing to pass through the Well of Eternity and enter the ravaged world. As his impossibly huge shadow drew ever closer to the Well's raging surface, Azshara gathered the most powerful of her high-borne followers. Only by linking their magics together, in one focused spell, would they be able to create a gateway large enough for Sargeras to enter.

Furion, convinced that the Well of Eternity was the demons' umbilical link to the physical world, insisted that it should be destroyed. His companions, knowing that the Well was the source of their immortality and powers, were shocked by the rash notion. Yet Tyrande, seeing the wisdom of Furion's theory, convinced Cenarius and their dragon comrades to storm Azshara's temple and find a way to shut the Well down for good.

Knowing that the Well's destruction would prevent him from ever wielding magic again, Illidan selfishly abandoned the group and set out to warn the high-borne of Furion's plan. Due to the madness brought on by his addiction and the stinging resentment towards his brother's affair with Tyrande, Illidan felt no remorse at betraying Furion and siding with Azshara and her ilk. Above all else, Illidan vowed to protect the Well's power by any means necessary.

Heartbroken by his brother's departure, Furion led his companions into the heart of Azshara's temple. Yet, as they stormed into the main audience chamber, they found the high-borne in the midst of their final dark incantation. The raging communal spell created an unstable vortex of power within the Well's raging depths. As Sargeras' ominous shadow drew ever closer to the surface, Furion and his allies rushed to attack.

Azshara, having received Illidan's warning, was more than prepared for them. Nearly all of Furion's followers fell before the mad Queen's raging powers. Tyrande, attempting to attack Azshara from behind, was caught off guard by the Queen's high-borne guardsmen. Though she vanquished the guardsmen, Tyrande suffered grievous wounds at their hands. At seeing his love fall, Furion went into a murderous rage and resolved to end Azshara's life.

As the battle raged inside and outside of the temple, Illidan appeared from the shadows near the shores of the great Well. Producing a set of specially crafted vials, Illidan knelt and filled each with the Well's shimmering waters. Convinced that the demons would crush the night elves' civilization, he planned to steal the sacred waters and keep their energies for himself.

The ensuing battle between Furion and Azshara threw the high-borne's carefully crafted spellwork into chaos. The unstable vortex within the Well's depths finally exploded and ignited a catastrophic chain of events that would sunder the world forever. The massive explosion rocked the temple to its foundations and sent massive quakes ripping through the tortured earth. As the horrific battle between the Legion and the night elves' allies raged around and above the ruined capital city, the surging Well of Eternity buckled in upon itself and collapsed.

The resultant catastrophic explosion shattered the earth and blotted out the skies...

Mount Hyjal and Illidan's Gift

As the aftershocks from the Well's implosion rattled the bones of the world, the seas rushed in to fill the gaping wound left in the earth. Nearly eighty percent of Kalimdor's landmass had been blasted apart, leaving only a handful of separate continents surrounding the new, raging sea. At the center of the new sea, where the Well of Eternity once stood, was a tumultuous storm of tidal fury and chaotic energies. This terrible scar, known as the Maelstrom, would never cease its furious spinning. It would remain a constant reminder of the terrible catastrophe and the utopian era that had been lost forever...

The few night elves that survived the horrific explosion rallied together on crudely made rafts and slowly made their way to the only landmass in sight. Somehow, by the graces of Elune, Furion, Tyrande and Cenarius had survived the Great Sundering. The weary heroes agreed to lead their fellow survivors and establish a new home for their people. As they journeyed in silence, they surveyed the wreckage of their world and realized that their passions had wrought the destruction all around them. Though Sargeras and his Legion had been ripped from the world by the Well's destruction, Furion and his companions were left to ponder the terrible cost of victory.

It was clear that Azshara and her elite high-borne followers had been smashed to the bottom of the raging sea. Still, there were many high-borne amongst the survivors who made their way to the shores of the new land. Though Furion mistrusted the high-bornes' motivations, he was satisfied that they could cause no real mischief without the Well's energies.

As the weary mass of night elves landed upon the shores of the new land, they found that the holy mountain, Hyjal, had survived the catastrophe. Seeking to establish a new home for themselves, Furion and the night elves climbed the slopes of Hyjal and reached its windswept summit. As they descended into the wooded bowl, nestled between the mountain's enormous peaks, they found a small, tranquil lake. To their horror, they found that the lake's waters had been fouled – by magic.

Illidan, having survived the Sundering as well, had reached Hyjal summit long before Furion and the night elves. In his mad bid to maintain the flows of magic in the world, Illidan had poured his vials, containing the precious waters from the Well of Eternity, into the mountain lake. The Well's potent energies quickly ignited and coalesced into a new Well of Eternity. The exultant Illidan, believing that the new Well was a gift to future generations, was shocked when Furion hunted him down. Furion explained to his brother that magic was innately chaotic and that its use would inevitably lead to widespread corruption and strife. Still, Illidan refused to relinquish his magical powers.

Knowing full well where Illidan's treacherous schemes would eventually lead, Furion decided to deal with his power-crazed brother once and for all. With Cenarius' help, Furion sealed Illidan within a vast underground chamber – to remain chained and powerless until the end of time. Concerned that destroying the new Well might bring about an even greater catastrophe, the night elves resolved to leave it be. However, Furion declared that they would never practice the arts of magic again. Under Cenarius' watchful eye, they began to study the ancient arts of druidism that would enable them to heal the ravaged earth and re-grow their beloved forests at the base of Mount Hyjal.

The World Tree and the Emerald Dream

For many years, the night elves worked tirelessly to rebuild what they could of their ancient homeland. Leaving their broken temples and roads to be overgrown, they constructed their new homes amidst the verdant trees and shadowed hills at Hyjal's base. In time, the dragons that had survived the great Sundering came forth from their secret abodes.

Alexstrasza the red, Ysera the green, and Nozdormu the bronze descended upon the druids' tranquil glades and surveyed the fruits of the night elves' labors. Furion, who had become an arch-druid of immense power, greeted the mighty dragons and told them about the creation of the new Well of Eternity. The great dragons were alarmed to hear the dark news and speculated that as long as the Well remained, the Legion might one day return and assault the world once again.

Furion and the three dragons made a pact to keep the Well safe and ensure that the agents of the Burning Legion would never find their way back into the world.

Alexstrasza, the Life-Giver, placed a single, enchanted acorn within the heart of the Well of Eternity. The acorn, activated by the potent, magical waters, sprung to life as a colossal tree. The mighty tree's roots grew from the Well's waters and its verdant canopy seemed to scrape the roof of the sky. The immense tree would be an everlasting symbol of the night elves' bond with nature, and its life-giving energies would extend out to heal the rest of the world over time. The night elves' named their World Tree, Nordrassil, which meant "crown of the heavens" in their native tongue.

Nozdormu, the Timeless, placed an enchantment upon the World Tree that ensured that as long as the colossal tree stood, the night elves would never age or fall prey to sickness or disease.

Ysera, the Dreamer, also placed an enchantment upon the World Tree by linking it to her own realm, the ethereal dimension known as the Emerald Dream. The Emerald Dream, a vast, ever-changing spirit world, existed outside the boundaries of the physical world. From the Dream, Ysera regulated the ebb and flow of nature and the evolutionary path of the world itself. The night elf druids, including Furion himself, were bound to the Dream through the World Tree. As part of the mystical pact, the druids agreed to sleep for centuries at a time so that their spirits could roam the infinite paths of Ysera's Dreamways. Though the druids were wary of losing so many years of their lives to hibernation, they selflessly agreed to uphold their bargain with Ysera.

Exile of the High Elves

As the centuries passed, the night elves' new society grew strong and expanded throughout the budding forest that they came to call Ashenvale. Many of the creatures and species that were abundant before the Great Sundering, such as furbolgs and quilboars, reappeared and flourished in the land. Under the druids' benevolent leadership, the night elves enjoyed an era of unprecedented peace and tranquility under the stars.

However, many of the original high-borne survivors grew restless. Like Illidan before them, they fell victim to the withdrawal that came from the loss of their coveted magics. They were tempted, once again, to tap the energies of the Well of Eternity and exult in their magical practices. Dath'Remar, the brash, outspoken leader of the high-borne, began to mock the druids publicly – calling them cowards for refusing to wield the magic that was theirs by right. Furion and the druids chaffed of Dath'Remar's arguments and warned the high-borne that any use of magic would be punishable by death. In their insolence, Dath'Remar and his followers unleashed a terrible magical storm upon Ashenvale in an ill-fated attempt to convince the druids to rescind their law.

The druids, unable to bring themselves to slaughter so many of their kin, decided to exile the reckless high-borne from their lands. Dath'Remar and his followers, glad to be rid of their conservative cousins at last, boarded a number of specially crafted ships and set sail upon the seas. Though none of them knew what awaited them beyond the waters of the raging Maelstrom, they were eager to establish their own homeland where they could practice their coveted magics with impunity. The high-borne, or 'Quel'dorei' as Azshara had named them in ages past, would eventually set shore upon the eastern land men would call Lordaeron. They planned to build their own magical kingdom - Quel'Thalas - and reject the night elves' precepts of moon worship and nocturnal activity. Forever after, they would be known only as the "high elves."

The Sentinels and the Long Vigil

With the departure of their wayward cousins, the night elves turned their attention back to the safekeeping of their enchanted homeland. The druids, sensing their time of hibernation nearing once again, prepared to sleep and leave their loved ones and families behind. Tyrande, who had become the First priestess of Elune, asked her love, Furion, not to leave her for Ysera's Emerald Dream. But, Furion, honor bound to enter the changing Dreamways, bid the priestess good-bye and swore that they would never be apart so long as they held true to their love.

Tyrande, left alone to protect Kalimdor from the dangers of the new world, assembled a powerful fighting force from amongst her night elf sisters. The fearless, highly trained warrior women who pledged themselves to Kalimdor's defense became known as the Sentinels. Though they preferred to patrol the shadowy forests of Ashenvale alone, they had many allies upon which they could call in times of urgency.

The demigod, Cenarius, remained nearby in the Moonglades of Mount Hyjal. His sons, known as the Keepers of the Grove, kept close watch on the night elves' land and regularly helped the Sentinels maintain peace in the land. Even Cenarius' shy daughters, the dryads, appeared in the open with increasing frequency.

Though the task of policing Ashenvale kept her busy, Tyrande felt lost and alone without Furion at her side. As the long centuries passed while the druids slept, her fears of a second demonic invasion grew more palpable. She could not shake the unnerving feeling that perhaps the Burning Legion was still out there, beyond the Great Dark of the sky plotting its revenge upon the night elves and the world of Azeroth.

NIGHT ELF HERO UNITS

Keeper of the Grove

The enchanted keepers are the favored sons of the demigod, Cenarius. Like their lesser dryad sisters, the keepers appear to be half night elf and half stag. They have enormous antlers and manes of leaves that flow down their backs. Their right hands are disfigured and twisted like the gnarled root-claws of the treants. Keepers possess many strange powers over nature and the animals. Though they typically remain within the sacred Moon Glades of Mount Hyjal, the keepers always heed the call to arms when the lands of Kalimdor are threatened.

ENTANGLING ROOTS

The sons of Cenarius are favored with the ability to cause roots to erupt from the ground and entrap enemy forces. These roots not only keep the enemy immobile, but also inflict damage.

FORCE OF NATURE

This ability allows the keeper to call forth allies from the surrounding forest. These stout treants will do as the keeper wills until the magic that animates them expires and the trees return once more to the earth.

THORNS AURA

While this aura is active, any forces that engage the keeper or his allies in hand to hand combat will be damaged by a druidic flurry of razor sharp thorns and brambles.

TRANQUILITY

In a demonstration of his ultimate communion with nature, the keeper may call down a mighty shower of rain that will restore health to all friendly forces within its range for its entire duration. The keeper is also healed by the majestic powers of nature that are unleashed.

Priestess of the Moon

The fearless leaders of the Sentinel army, the priestesses of the moon epitomize the power and grace of their race's ancient moon goddess, Elune. The priestesses, equipped with silvery, glowing armor, ride the fearless Frostsaber tigers of Winterspring into battle. Charged with the safekeeping of the night elf lands and armed with magical energy bows, the priestesses will stop at nothing to rid their ancient land of evil.

SHADOWMELD

Empowered by the goddess Elune, night elf warriors possess the ability to completely blend in with their surroundings between sunset and sunrise, rendering them invisible to their enemy. This effect, however, can only be achieved while the warriors are standing completely still.

SCOUT

The scout is an owl that may be sent to any area of the map for observation purposes and to reveal invisible enemies. The owl will only reveal for a limited amount of time.

SEARING ARROWS

Calling upon the powers of the Moon Goddess Elune to imbue her arrows with searing magical energy, the priestess is able to fire deadly volleys at any foe.

TRUESHOT AURA

The commanding presence of the priestess boosts the morale of her warriors, enabling their attacks to strike with heightened accuracy and power.

STARFALL

At the peak of her experience, the priestess may call down a furious shower of falling stars that cause massive destruction amongst enemy forces. This catastrophic power, given to the priestess by Elune herself, achieves its full duration as long as the priestess stays in the spell's vicinity.

Demon Hunter

Demon hunters are dark, shadowy warriors who are shunned by the greater night elf society. They made a pact, long ago, to fight against the forces of chaos using its own terrible powers against it. These mysterious warriors ritually blind themselves so that they develop spectral sight that enables them to see demons and undead with greater clarity. They wield demonically charged warblades in battle and even call upon demonic energies to augment their formidable combat skills. Although they are counted as some of the mightiest warriors within the night elves' society, the demon hunters are always maligned and misunderstood for making their selfless pact with darkness.

EVASION
With evasion, the demon hunter gains the advantage of being able to dodge enemy strikes. Although this does not work against every strike, it is nonetheless a powerful defensive tactic.

IMMOLATION
The demon hunter's mastery of dark powers allows him to create a fiery shell around his body that inflicts damage on nearby enemies. This ability, however, takes tremendous concentration to use and will quickly drain the demon hunter of power if used too often.

MANA BURN
The demon hunter may channel his demonic energies into a bolt of negative energy that will burn away an enemy's mana reserves.

METAMORPHOSIS
At the height of his powers, the demon hunter may change into demon form for a limited amount of time. While in this form the demon hunter not only possesses the ability to hurl fireballs, but also enjoys increased regeneration and health.

Night Elf Units

Wisp
Wisps are ancient spirits of nature that inhabit the forestlands of Kalimdor. Legends say that Wisps are actually the disembodied spirits of deceased night elves, but these rumors have yet to be proven. The wisps act in unison with the night elves and serve to strengthen the demigod-like trees known as the Ancients. Beckoned by the night elves, Wisps are capable of animating various trees and expanding themselves into rough-hewn structures of living wood and stone.

DETONATE
All Wisps possess the ability to self-terminate, negating any magical effects in the immediate area, and draining enemy forces within the vicinity of mana.

RENEW
This ability allows the wisp to use its healing powers to mend friendly night elf structures and mechanical units. This ability costs a minimal amount of gold and lumber.

Archer
Archers compose the first rank of the Sentinel army. These brave warrior women are expert marksmen and use the concealing forests of Kalimdor to their advantage. Their lightning-quick ambushes are legendary, for few warriors can match the proud archers' speed and cunning. Like all night elf women, archers have the ability to Shadowmeld at night.

SHADOWMELD

Empowered by the goddess Elune, night elf warriors possess the ability to completely blend in with their surroundings between sunset and sunrise, rendering them invisible to their enemy. This effect, however, can only be achieved while the warriors are standing completely still.

Huntress

Huntresses are the elite cadre of the Sentinel army. Drawing their strength from the moon goddess, Elune, these warrior women ride the feral Nightsaber panthers into battle. Huntresses are strong and swift, and merciless to those who would defile the sanctity of Ashenvale Forest. Like all night elf women, Huntresses are able to Shadowmeld at night.

SHADOWMELD

Empowered by the goddess Elune, night elf warriors possess the ability to completely blend in with their surroundings between sunset and sunrise, rendering them invisible to their enemy. This effect, however, can only be achieved while the warriors are standing completely still.

SENTINEL

This ability enables the huntress to see through the eyes of her owl familiar, allowing her to spy on enemy positions. The owl will perch at a tree permanently, unless the tree is destroyed.

Dryad

The enchanted dryads are the daughters of the demigod, Cenarius. The playful, frolicking creatures vaguely resemble centaurs (their cursed cousins), but have bodies more akin to woodland fauns. Swift and sure, the dryads are at peace with all of the children of the forest. Though they abhor unnecessary violence, the dryads will defend the wildlands of Kalimdor with their lives if need be.

ABOLISH MAGIC

The daughters of Cenarius can gain the ability to abolish all harmful magic and undo the works of enemy sorcerers who recklessly wield their powers in an affront to nature.

MAGIC IMMUNITY

With this ability, the dryad herself is immune to magic in all forms. This is an innate ability that does not rely upon stored mana and does not diminish over time.

Druid of the Claw

These ancient druids have adopted the totem of the bear and use the powers of their totem to defend their society from any external threats. When not in hibernation, they are fond of assuming bear form and roaming in seclusion throughout the wildlands of Kalimdor. When riled, the druids of the claw display ferocious power and stamina. Their magical spells augment their allies' fighting skills and bravery as well.

BEAR FORM

The power of their spirit totem allows the druids of the claw to assume the form of a mighty bear. In battle, the ferocity of these beasts is legendary.

REJUVENATION

This power allows the druid of the claw to heal over time. This ability may be used on the druid himself, or on nearby allies who have been wounded over the course of battle.

ROAR

Tapping into the primal forces of nature and the raw power of his totem, the druid of the claw can roar during battle, encouraging his allies to inflict increased damage upon the enemy.

Druid of the Talon

These secretive druids have adopted the totem of the storm crow. Their primary role in society is information gathering and intelligence. They have the ability to transform into storm crows and fly over the field of battle to scout and deliver orders to distant troops. Their magical abilities are capable of channeling even the winds to fight against the enemies of Kalimdor.

CROW FORM

The druid of the talon may use the power of his spirit totem to transform into a giant storm crow. While in this form, the druid can fly, enabling him to cross almost any terrain.

CYCLONE

Using his totem's power to channel the chaotic forces of the wind, the druid of the talon may create a furious cyclone that will lift enemy forces high into the air and then drop them back onto the ground, where they will be slowed for a limited amount of time.

FAERIE FIRE

This ability, when cast, strips an enemy unit of its armor for a limited duration of time. While the spell is active, the druid may observe the enemy no matter how great a distance may separate them.

Treant

Treants are enormous enchanted beings whose bodies are born of the living trees of Kalimdor. They guard the forests of Kalimdor and are counted as some of the eldest beings alive. Treants are tremendously strong and resilient to even the strongest blows. In time of peril, they can be seen emerging from their shadowy forests to protect the land from evil and corruption.

Hippogryph

Hippogryphs are ancient, magical beasts whose bodies resemble both stags and ravens. They patrol the skies above Kalimdor and viciously attack any enemies of the wilds that they encounter. The intelligent hippogryphs have given their allegiance to the night elves in honor of Cenarius, demigod, who stands as the protector of nature and all of its creatures.

Hippogryph Rider

In the heat of battle, night elf archers can call upon the mighty hippogryphs to carry them into the air. The archers who mount the flying beasts are capable of firing their arrows from the hippogryphs' backs. The brave creatures respond to the female riders as if they shared an empathic bond.

Chimaera

The mysterious chimaeras of Ashenvale Forest are deadly, territorial beasts who have developed an empathic bond with the night elf race. The fearsome, two-headed chimaeras fly above the dark forests spewing forth their terrible breath upon all who would defy the sanctity of Kalimdor. Just the sight of these dark, massive beasts is enough to drive most enemies to retreat.

Ballistae

Crafted from the sturdy ashenwood trees, the night elves' ballistae are deadly siege machines built to fling heavy bolts of ironwood at both enemy forces and structures. Ballistae are considered an invaluable asset to the night elf Sentinels due to their mobility and accuracy in tense combat situations.

Night Elf Structures

Tree of Life

The mighty tree of life is an enchanted sapling of the World Tree, Nordrassil, from which the night elves draw their life energies. This mysterious ancient is the key to the night elves' immortality and harmonious coexistence with nature. Nordrassil's energy, channeled through the tree of life, allows the night elves to benefit from its powers regardless of the vast distances that might separate them.

EAT TREE

The night elf ancients possess the ability to consume nearby trees to restore vital health. When ancients are being attacked, resorting to this technique can prove to be a powerful healing tactic.

UPROOT

All ancients may root and uproot. This ability provides the ancients with the mobility to either attack or relocate when the need arises.

ENTANGLE GOLD MINE

It is necessary for the tree of life to entangle a gold mine with its massive

roots before nearby wisps will be able to harvest from it. As long as the mine is entangled, gold from the mine may be processed to fuel the night elf economy.

Moon Well

Moon Wells are hallowed repositories of the sacred waters of the Well of Eternity, the pool of energy that gives life to the mystical World Tree. When additional water is added, these wells nourish the night elf troops with their life sustaining waters. Additional moon wells become necessary as the night elf forces grow in number.

REPLENISH MANA AND LIFE

Using the concentrated waters of the Well of Eternity, Moon Wells can replenish both the mana and health of friendly forces that drink from it. At nighttime, the well's waters regenerate to be used again the next day.

Ancient of War

Embodied in this ancient guardian are the spirits of courage and determination that are necessary to propel the will of the night elves. Calling upon the long-forgotten energies of conflicts from ages past, this guardian provides a link to the brutal side of nature and the cycle of life and death that rules all creation.

EAT TREE

The night elf ancients possess the ability to consume nearby trees to restore vital health. When being attacked, resorting to this technique can prove to be a powerful healing tactic.

UPROOT

All ancients may root and uproot. This ability provides the ancients with the mobility to either attack or relocate when the need arises.

Hunter's Hall

This hall is a place where the materials of war are imbued with the night elves' mystical enhancements. Wood and steel are fashioned into the stout armor using established traditions and methods stretching back thousands of years, as the spirits of the Ancient Guardians are invoked and their blessings bestowed upon each completed work.

Ancient Protector

The early purpose of these primeval guardians was to defend the resting places of the druids as they slept. Called now into service for the Third War, these wardens dedicate their existence to the defense of their brethren and the forested lands of Ashenvale. These mighty ancients can also hurl enormous boulders at any enemies who threaten the tranquility of the night elves' villages.

EAT TREE

The night elf ancients possess the ability to consume nearby trees to restore vital health. When being attacked, resorting to this technique can prove to be a powerful healing tactic.

UPROOT

All ancients may root and uproot. This ability provides the ancients with the mobility to either attack or relocate when the need arises.

Tree of Ages

With the passage of time, a tree of life may grow into a tree of ages, tempering the balance of nature and forging a bond strong enough to allow advanced development within the night elf community. With this evolution comes increased knowledge, wisdom and awareness.

EAT TREE

The night elf ancients possess the ability to consume nearby trees to restore vital health. When being attacked, resorting to this technique can prove to be a powerful healing tactic.

UPROOT

All ancients may root and uproot. This ability provides the ancients with the mobility to either attack or relocate when the need arises.

Ancient of Wind

Ancients of the wind are able to tap into the more feral side of nature. The ancient of the wind allows contact with the stoic druids of the talon. This site also provides a location for the taming of the mighty hippogryphs.

EAT TREE

The night elf ancients possess the ability to consume nearby trees to restore vital health. When being attacked, resorting to this technique can prove to be a powerful healing tactic.

UPROOT

All ancients may root and uproot. This ability provides the ancients with the mobility to either attack or relocate when the need arises.

Ancient of Lore

The ancients of lore are the keepers of wisdom, and the living keys necessary to unlock nature's most guarded secrets. Contact with the venerated druids of the claw is only made possible through the existence of this enlightened sentinel. The knowledge of this ancient is necessary also to enable communion with the enigmatic, free-spirited dryads.

EAT TREE

The night elf ancients possess the ability to consume nearby trees to restore vital health. When being attacked, resorting to this technique can prove to be a powerful healing tactic.

UPROOT

All ancients may root and uproot. This ability provides the ancients with the mobility to either attack or relocate when the need arises.

Altar of Elders

So powerful is the night elf bond with nature, that even upon their death, their life energies may be recalled, and their spirit made tangible in the waking world once again. For this to occur, a nexus must be constructed, a channeling place to collect and restore life energies. This place is the altar of elders.

Tree of Eternity

Once a tree of ages reaches its full maturity, it evolves into a tree of eternity. This is the highest level of growth, and the strongest possible bond with the World Tree and the Well of Eternity. At this point the night elf community is at its height, drawing freely from the tree's nearly unlimited power.

Chimaera Roost

Only with the evolution of the tree of eternity do the feral chimaeras feel content to allow for training and enhancement through night elf intervention. This kinship is necessary to fully realize the benefits of the chimaera alliance.

To Quel'Thalas
Tirisfal Glades
Lordaeron
Capital City
Stratholme
Mardenholde Keep
Hearthglen
Brill
Darrowmere Lake
Caer Darrow
Lordamere Lake
Fenris Isle
Alterac Ruins
Andorhal
Alterac
Strahnbrad
Internment Camp
Internment Camp
Durnhold Keep
Internment Camp
Orc Village
Aerie Peak
Alterac Mountains
The Violet Citadel
Stromgarde
Dalaran

Sunwell Grove
Silvermoon
Quel'Thalas
Runestone
Inner Elfgate
Runestone
Outer Elfgate
Runestone
Runestone
Runestone
Lake Abasi
To Lordaeron
Ziggurat
Zul'aman
Darrowmere Lake
Caer Darrow
Tyr's Hand

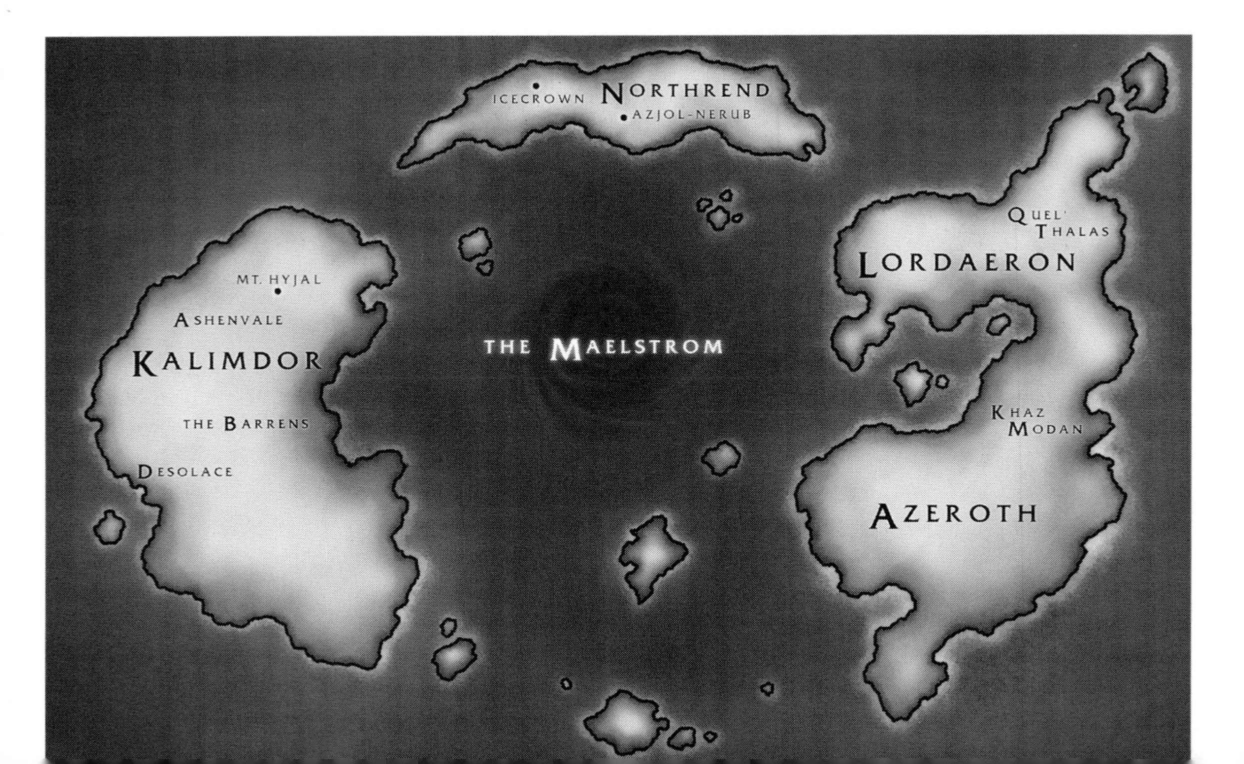
Northrend
Icecrown
Azjol-Nerub
Quel'Thalas
Lordaeron
Mt. Hyjal
Ashenvale
Kalimdor
The Maelstrom
The Barrens
Khaz Modan
Desolace
Azeroth

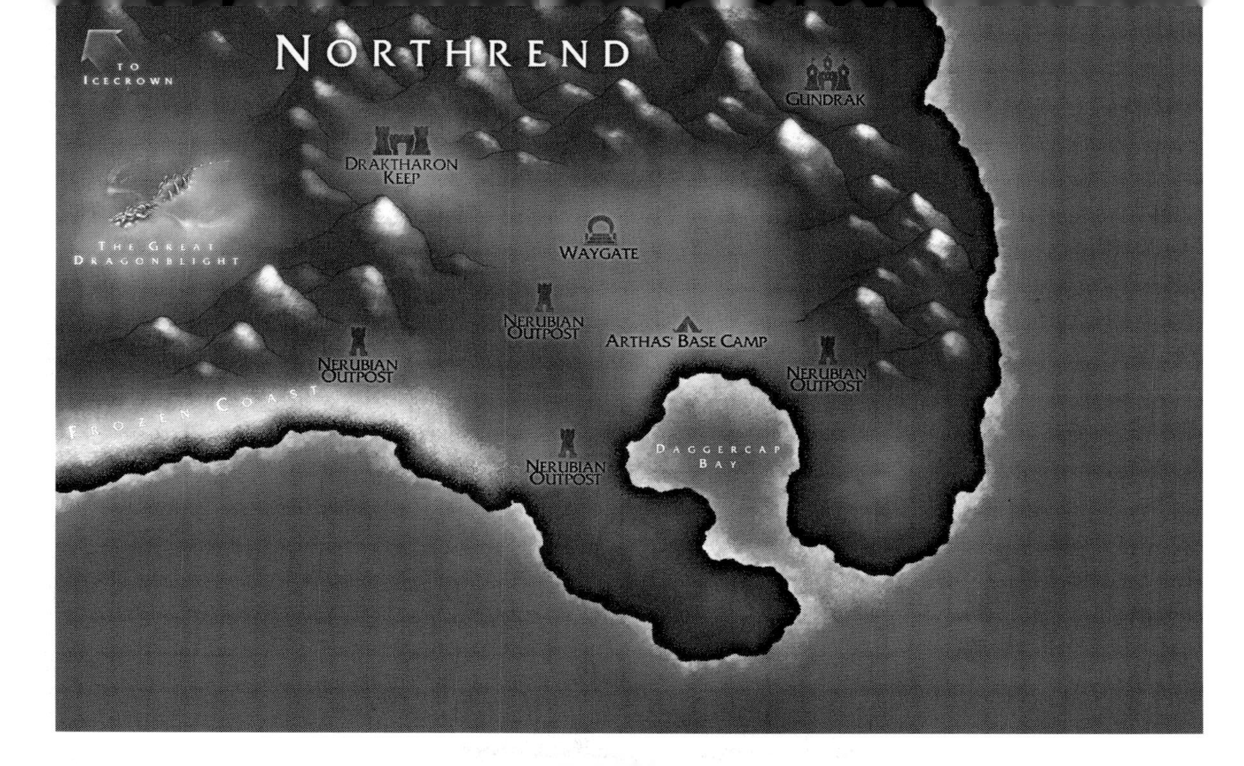
NORTHREND
TO ICECROWN
GUNDRAK
DRAKTHARON KEEP
WAYGATE
THE GREAT DRAGONBLIGHT
NERUBIAN OUTPOST
ARTHAS' BASE CAMP
NERUBIAN OUTPOST
NERUBIAN OUTPOST
FROZEN COAST
NERUBIAN OUTPOST
DAGGERCAP BAY

Darkshore
Furbolg Camp
Ancient Ruins
Ancient Ruins
Furbolg Camp
The World Tree
Winterspring
Well of Eternity
Barrow Dens
Furbolg Camp
Mount Hyjal
Grove of Cenarius
Felwood
Moonglade
Furbolg Camp
Dryad Shrine
Ancient Ruins
Ashenvale Forest
Furbolg Camp
To The Barrens

TO ASHENVALE
STONETALON PEAK
HARPY NEST
HARPY NEST
HARPY NEST
RAZORFEN DOWNS
QUILLBOAR CAMP
QUILLBOAR CAMP
THE BARRENS
TAUREN CAMP
TAUREN CAMP
MULGORE
QUILLBOAR CAMP
TAUREN CAMP
DESOLACE
THRALL'S LANDING SITE
TAUREN CAMP
TAUREN CAMP

METZEN

Origin of the Burning Legion

The Titans and the Ordering

No one knows exactly how the universe began. Some theorize that a catastrophic cosmic explosion sent the infinite worlds spinning out into the vastness of the Great Dark – worlds that would one day bear life-forms of wondrous and terrible diversity. Others believe that the universe, at it exists, was created as a whole by a singular, all-powerful entity. Though the exact origins of the chaotic universe remain unclear, it is clear that a race of powerful beings arose to bring order to the various worlds and ensure a safe future for the beings that would follow in their footsteps.

The Titans, colossal, metallic-skinned gods from the far reaches of the cosmos, came forward and set to work on the worlds they encountered. They shaped the form of their worlds by raising mighty mountains and dredging out vast seas. They breathed skies and raging atmospheres into being – all part of their unfathomable, far-sighted plan to create order out of chaos. They even empowered primitive races to tend to their works and maintain the integrity of their respective worlds.

The Titans, ruled by an elite sect known as the Pantheon, brought order to a hundred million worlds scattered throughout the Great Dark Beyond during the first ages of creation. The benevolent Pantheon, seeking to safeguard their structured worlds, was ever vigilant against the threat of attack from the vile, extra-dimensional entities of the Twisting Nether. The Nether, an ethereal dimension of chaotic magics that connected the myriad worlds of the universe together, was home to an infinite number of malefic, demonic beings, who sought only to destroy life and devour the energies of the living universe. The pure-hearted, altruistic Titans, unable to conceive of evil or wickedness in any form, struggled to find a way to end the demons' constant threat.

Sargeras and the Betrayal

To combat the demonic entities that made their way into the Titans' worlds from the Twisting Nether, the Pantheon elected their greatest warrior, Sargeras, to act as their first line of defense. Sargeras, a noble giant of molten bronze, carried out his duties for countless millennia, seeking out and destroying the demons wherever he could find them. Over the eons, Sargeras encountered two powerful demonic races, both of which were bent on gaining power and dominance over the physical universe.

The Eredar, an insidious race of devilish sorcerers, used their warlock magics to enslave a number of worlds that they had invaded. The indigenous races of those worlds were mutated by the Eredar's chaotic powers and turned into demons themselves. Though Sargeras' nearly limitless powers were more than enough to defeat the vile Eredar, he was greatly troubled by the creatures' corruption and all-consuming evil. Unable to fathom such depravity and spite, the great Titan slipped into a brooding depression. Despite his growing unease, Sargeras sought to rid the universe of the warlocks for all time, by trapping them within a vacuous corner of the Twisting Nether.

As his confusion and depression deepened, Sargeras was forced to contend with another group intent on disrupting the Titans' order. The Nathrezim, a dark race of vampiric demons (also known as Dreadlords) set out to conquer a populated world by possessing its inhabitants and turning them to the shadow. The nefarious, scheming Dreadlords had turned whole nations against one another by manipulating them through unthinking hatred and mistrust. Though Sargeras defeated the Nathrezim easily, their corruption affected him deeply.

The noble Sargeras, unable to process the raging doubt and despair that overwhelmed his senses, lost all faith in not only his mission, but the Titans' vision of an ordered universe, as well. Sargeras began to believe that the concept of order itself was folly – and that chaos and depravity were the only absolutes within the dark, lonely universe. Though his fellow Titans tried to persuade him of his error and console his raging emotions, he disregarded their theories as delusional. Storming from their ranks forever, Sargeras set out to find his own place in the universe. Though the Pantheon was sorrowful for his departure, they would never believe just how far their lost brother would go.

As Sargeras' madness consumed the last vestiges of his noble spirit, he began to rationalize that the Titans were truly responsible for creation's failure. Deciding, at last, to undo their works throughout the universe, he set out to form an unstoppable army that would set the physical universe to the flame.

Even Sargeras' titanic form distorted from the corruption that plagued his once noble heart. His eyes, hair and beard erupted in flames and his bronze, metallic skin split open to reveal an endless furnace of hate and flame.

In his madness, Sargeras shattered the prisons of the Eredar and the Nathrezim and set the vile demons free. The cunning demons, bowing before the dark Titan's vast rage and power, offered themselves to him and swore to serve him in whatever malicious way they could. From the ranks of the powerful Eredar, Sargeras chose two champions to lead his demonic army of destruction.

Kil'jaeden the Deceiver was chosen to seek out the darkest races in the universe and lure them to Sargeras' shadow. The second champion, Archimonde the Defiler, was chosen to lead Sargeras' vast armies into battle against any who would stand against the dark Titan's will.

Kil'jaeden's first move was to enslave the vampiric Dreadlords under his terrible power. The Dreadlords, serving as his elite guard and agents throughout the universe, took pleasure in their work by locating primitive races for their master to corrupt and bring into the fold. First amongst the Dreadlords was Tichondrius the Darkener. Tichondrius served Kil'jaeden as the perfect soldier and agreed to promote Sargeras' burning will to all the dark corners of the universe.

The mighty Archimonde also empowered agents of his own. Calling upon the malefic Pit Lords and their barbarous leader, Mannoroth, he hoped to forge a fighting elite that would scour creation of all life.

Sargeras, seeing that his armies were amassed and ready to follow his every command, launched his raging forces into the vastness of the Great Dark. He referred to his growing army as the Burning Legion. To this date, it is still unclear as to how many worlds they consumed and burned on their unholy crusade across the universe.

The Ordering of Azeroth

Apparently unaware of Sargeras' mission to undo their myriad works, the Titans continued to move from world to world, shaping and ordering them as they saw fit. Along their journey they came across a small world that's inhabitants would later name Azeroth. As the Titans made their way across the chaotic, primordial landscape, they encountered a number of hostile, elemental beings. The elementals, worshipping a race of unfathomable evil beings known only as the Old Gods, vowed to drive the Titans back and keep their world inviolate from the invaders' metallic touch.

The Pantheon, troubled by the Old Gods' penchant for evil, sent their forces to make war upon the elementals and their dark masters. Though the elementals fought and raged, their powers could not stop the mighty Titans. The Pantheon shattered the Old Gods' citadels and chained the five evil beings far beneath the surface of the world. Without the Old Gods' power to keep their raging spirits bound to the physical world, the elementals dissipated and bled back into the earth itself. With the elementals' departure, nature calmed, and the world settled into a peaceful harmony. The Titans, seeing that the threat was contained, set to work.

The Titans empowered a number of races to help them fashion the world. To help them dredge out the fathomless caverns beneath the earth, they created the dwarves from magical, living stone. To help them dredge out the seas and lift the land from the sea floor, they created the immense, but gentle sea giants. For many ages the Titans moved and shaped the earth, until at last, there remained only one perfect continent. At the continent's center, the Titans crafted a lake of scintillating energies. The lake, that they named the Well of Eternity, was to be the fount of life for the world. Its potent energies would nurture the bones of the world and empower life to take root in the land's rich soil. Over time, plants, trees, monsters and creatures of every kind began to thrive on the primordial continent. As twilight fell on the final day of their labors, the Titans named the continent Kalimdor – "land of a eternal starlight."

Satisfied that the small world had been ordered and that their work was done, the Titans prepared to leave Azeroth behind. Yet, before they departed, they decided to empower the greatest newborn species of the world to watch over Kalimdor should any force ever threaten its perfect tranquility. Each remaining member of the Pantheon imbued a portion of its power to the five great dragons awoken in that mythic age. Alexstrasza the Life-Binder, Malygos the Spell-Weaver, Ysera the Dreamer, Nozdormu the Timeless, and Neltharion the Earth-Warder were all empowered by the Titans' vast powers and charged with the world's defense.

With the dragons prepared to safeguard their creation, the Titans left Azeroth behind forever. Unfortunately for them, and the small, newborn world they had shaped, it was only a matter of time before Sargeras learned of its existence…

Demon Units

Felhound

Felhounds are demon hounds used by the Pit Lords to sniff out sources of magic wherever they be found. Felhounds, who feed upon magic itself, are fond of draining the energies of hapless wizards and then ripping their bodies to shreds.

Warlock

Born of the Eredar race, warlocks are absolutely corrupt and unimaginably powerful. Their chaos magics have burnt out whole worlds and annihilated countless species over the aeons. Kil'jaeden taught the orcs the secrets of warlock magics, but the orcs could never master the powers of entropy and destruction as well as the wicked Eredar. Under Archimonde's command, the warlocks serve as the Legion's tacticians and strategists.

Doom Guard

The fearsome Doom Guard serve as Archimonde's personal escorts. Although they are often called upon to perform a number of duties for the Legion, their loyalty lies with him alone. These monstrous, fiery warriors are nearly immune to magic and can defeat entire armies with their sheer strength alone.

Pit Lord

The Pit Lords who serve under Mannoroth the Destructor are some of the most cruel, barbarous butchers to ever roam the trackless wastes of the Twisting Nether. These hulking engines of hate and death love only to kill and bring sorrow to all living creatures. Fanatically loyal to Mannoroth, the Pit Lords will stop at nothing to see the will of the Legion upheld.

Infernal

These mindless giants of flame and fury are summoned by the warlocks' Inferno spell. Falling to earth as green, molten meteorites, infernals exist only to destroy every living thing in their path. Though their lifespans are limited, the mighty infernals have been known to destroy entire cities before their energies dissipated back into the Great Dark Beyond.

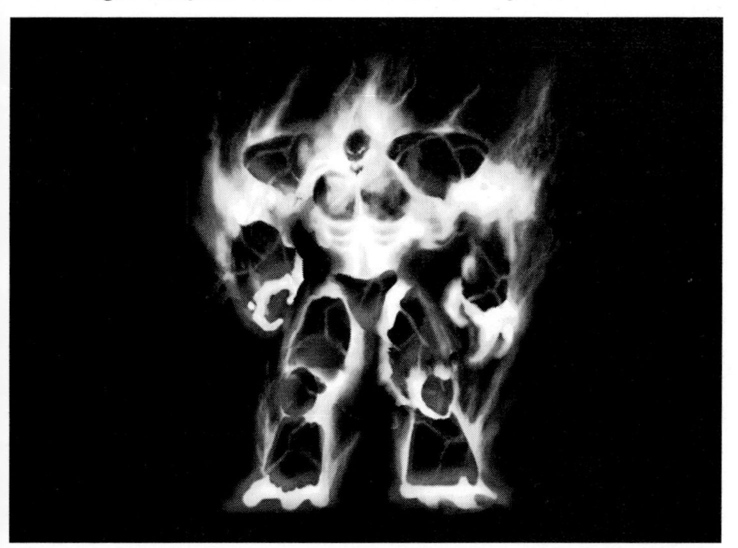

Creatures of Lordaeron & Northrend

Bandits

Human bandits prey upon hapless travelers and soldiers alike. These lawless rogues think only of theft and burglary and enjoy causing great pain to their victims as well. Though the Alliance has offered large bounties towards the capture of these wretched men, they always find a way to slink back into the shadows of the wilds.

Dragons, Blue

The blue Dragonflight, ruled by Malygos, the lord of magic, was all but devastated by the evil Deathwing and his black Dragonflight. Though there are few great blue dragons left in the world, their magical powers are awesome to behold. Native to Northrend, the few blues stay relatively close to the great Dragonblight, where they commune with the ancient dragon spirits who died in ages past. Their freezing breath and gargantuan claws have been the death of many hapless travelers in Northrend.

Dragons, Red

The red Dragonflight, ruled by the Dragonqueen, Alexstrasza, is a noble and honorable group of creatures. They consider themselves the protectors of all life, and in many ways they are. More often than not, they are found protecting sacred areas and items, seeking to keep them from lesser beings who might be hurt by their energies. Their breath is a fearsome stream of fire, and they have been known to swallow enemies whole and slowly digest them over the course of a day. Their most hated enemies are the black dragons ruled by the great, dark leviathan, Deathwing.

Fallen Priest

These wretched individuals were once counted as the most devout amongst the clergy of Lordaeron. But, after years of constant war and suffering, they have lost their sense of the holy Light. Now they exist only to spread their frustration and negativity to their fellow men and women.

Ghost

Ghosts are tortured spirits who writhe in the agony of undeath. Unable to realize that are no longer alive, they roam the trackless wastes between the Twisting Nether and the physical world, seeking release from their eternal suffering. Though they are not necessarily evil, they hunger for physical contact, often causing great harm to any living beings they touch.

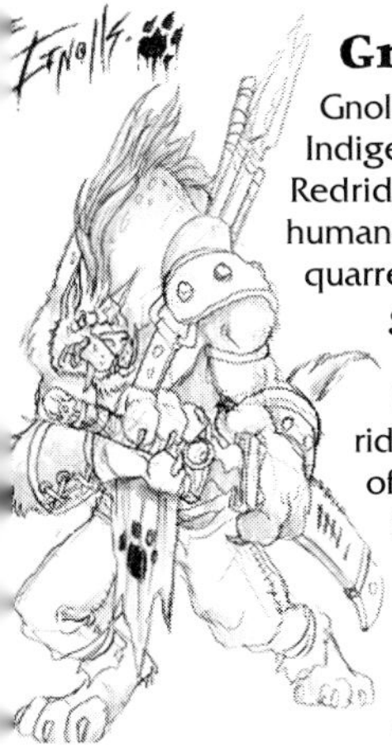

Gnolls

Gnolls are one of the younger races of Lordaeron. Indigenous to both the Alterac Mountains and the Redridge Range far to the south, these hyena-like humanoids are extremely aggressive and are often found quarreling amongst themselves. Though relatively intelligent compared to most beasts, they are not very bright by human standards. They have been known to manipulate each other into fights over ridiculous things like "whose shadow is larger." It has often been stated that the gnolls would be quite a fearsome race, if they ever stopped tearing each other to pieces long enough to organize themselves into an army.

Golems

Golems are magically wrought automatons of varying types of stone. Most Golems can be found in and around Dalaran, for the mages there created them to perform manual labor and guard their mystical holdings. Certain renegade wizards have also been known to create their own Golems to protect their secret dens and lairs. Most Golems are magically protected from spells, so that enemy mages cannot turn them against their creators. Golems are generally thought to be mindless. However, there have been documented cases of Golems roaming freely, without their masters to control them. Where these vagabond constructs go or what they seek is a complete mystery.

Kobolds

Kobolds are a race of sniveling, rat-like humanoids who infest the deep tunnels of the Alterac and Redridge Mountains. Cowardly and pathetic by nature, they can be riled to action when backed into a corner. Kobolds have limited intelligence and usually try to stay away from populated areas where other, larger races dwell.

Murlocs

Though relatively new to Lordaeron, it is purported that Murlocs are actually a very ancient race of Azeroth. These creatures have steadily been moving in-land from their oceanic dwelling places, even adapting to fresh-water lakes and rivers in order to populate areas they would not normally be found in. Though they continue to inhabit more areas of Lordaeron, their supposed intelligence is debatable due to the fact that their guttural language is impossibly difficult to decipher. However, their use of weaponry and uncanny fighting abilities imply a rather sinister racial intellect.

Nerubians

The Nerubian spider-men once ruled over the kingdom of Azjol-Nerub that stretched like a great web beneath the desolate glaciers of Northrend. However, the Lich King crushed their dark empire and sent them skittering into the arctic wastelands. Though there are few pockets of Nerubian warriors left, they still seek to gain vengeance upon Ner'zhul and reclaim their subterranean kingdom.

Ogres

Ogres are one of the few races that are not indigenous to Azeroth. They were actually brought from the world of Draenor during the First War a generation ago. Ogres are not the stupid, lumbering two-headed beasts they once seemed to be. In fact, many of the ogre lords have rallied the remnants of their people that were scattered when the horde fell. Though their plans are unknown, there is no doubt that these powerful, deceptively intelligent warriors will gather their forces once more.

Revenants

Revenants are hateful undead creatures who outside the domain of Ner'zhul's control. Bonded to base elemental spirits, these phantom creatures live only to rage and use their powers for destruction.

Trolls, Forest

Forest trolls are one of the most ancient indigenous races of Lordaeron whose civilization actually predates that of the high elves by several thousand years. They are vile creatures for the most part, practicing voodoo, ritual sacrifices, and in some cases - though never documented, cannibalism. Though forest trolls are never friendly, they have a particular hatred for the high elves, whom they consider the despoilers of their ancient homelands. However, their hatred does end with the elves, they hold all the races in contempt and will only work with others if it means the possible elimination of a more hated enemy. The forest trolls worked briefly with the orcish horde during the Second War, but quickly abandoned their orcish allies after the horde's defeat.

Trolls, Ice

Like their evil forest troll cousins, ice trolls revel in carnage and wickedness. Driven into the desolate wastes of Northrend in ancient times, the ice trolls carved out a meager society for themselves amongst the cold stone and lifeless plains. Cannibalistic by nature, ice trolls are renowned for their love of eating their recently slain enemies raw. Their social structure is very similar to that of their forest dwelling cousins.

Wendigo

The indigenous wendigo of Northrend are exceedingly voracious creatures. Solitary by nature, wendigo rarely live amongst others of their kind. Cannibalistic and savage, these hulking, fur-covered humanoids are highly territorial and do not take kindly to intruders stumbling into their hunting grounds.

Wizards

Though most contemporary human and high elven mages bow to the sovereignty of Dalaran and the Kirin Tor, there are a great many who choose to delve into the secrets of magic by themselves. Considered to be non-sanctioned renegades by the Kirin Tor, these rogue mages strive to expand their knowledge of magic and spellcraft beyond the constraints of what most other wizards believe to be safe or morally acceptable.

Wolves

Wolves are indigenous to many parts of Azeroth. They live on every known continent and have a wide variety of sub-species and social habits. Though most wolves are hostile towards humans and demi-humans who encroach upon their territories, there are a few unique wolf packs who have befriended demi-human counterparts (like the orcs, for example).

The Creatures of Kalimdor

Corrupted Treants

These wretched tree-creatures were once proud, immortal defenders of Ashenvale forest. Yet, when the Burning Legion invaded the world in ages past, its demonic energies corrupted many of the ancient tree-men and drove them into shadow. Now these tortured creatures live only to spread their corruption and hatred of all living things.

Dragons, Black

Though the black Dragonflight was nearly annihilated in ages past, a few of the evil creatures have made their homes in the dry, desolate wastes of the Barrens. With their lord, Deathwing, either missing or dead, the black dragons seek to appease only themselves. The creatures are immensely powerful and cruel and revel in mortal suffering. The black dragons are the enemies of every other Dragonflight, especially the great red dragons of Lordaeron.

Dragons, Green

The enchanted, ethereal green dragons live only to serve the forces of nature and uphold the balance between mortal creatures and the ever-evolving world. The green Dragonflight, ruled by the dreaming goddess, Ysera, holds a special love for the night elves and their druids. Though most green dragons live within the mystical dimension known as the Emerald Dream, a few of the graceful creatures still roam the shadowy paths of Ashenvale forest.

Centaur

Legend holds that the primitive, barbaric centaurs are actually the bastard off-spring of the night elf demigod, Cenarius. Whether or not this is true, it is certain that they are savagery and brutality incarnate. These horse-men ceaselessly terrorize the Barrens of Kalimdor and maraud the villages and cities of the lands indigenous peoples. The tauren claim that the centaur have always existed to scourge the land.

Furbolgs

Furbolgs are hulking, simple-minded bear-men who live within the savage corners of Ashenvale forest. Though they have no special love for war or murder, their tribes have become increasingly hostile as of late. The night elves, concerned by the once peaceful race's condition, have attempted to help the furbolgs settle their tensions. But the mighty bear-men retreat ever-further into their territories and fall deeper into the rage that is overtaking their race.

Harpies

These vile, unscrupulous winged women live only to cause mischief and sorrow. Hailing from the windy Stonetalon Mountains, the harpies are masterful at ambushing hapless caravans and foolish travelers alike.

Salamanders

These subterranean beasts share a common ancestry with the mighty kodo beasts. However, they have adapted to life beneath the earth by evolving a number of natural defenses and abilities.

Kodos

The giant, slow-moving kodo beasts of the Barrens are one of the most intriguing species of Kalimdor. Though gentle and ponderous by nature, these mighty beasts become fierce enemies when threatened or attacked. Many kodos hold a special bond with the benevolent tauren race.

It is said that some rare kodos are bound to the spirits of the sky and storm. Thus, the tauren have legends about those they call Lightning Lizards, Thunder Lizards and Storm Walkers. Whether or not these behemoths actually have supernatural powers remains to be seen.

Mutant Murlocs

Though Murlocs abound along the rugged coastal regions of Kalimdor, there is a mutant strain of the race that has emerged in recent months. Though it is unclear what has caused the creature's strange mutations, many agree that something dark and sinister is awakening deep beneath the raging Maelstrom. The mutant Murlocs have been so corrupted that they have been known to turn on their own brethren under duress.

Owlbears

These lumbering, misshapen creatures are beloved by the night elf druids and treants alike. They are benevolent by nature, but fearsome when roused or angered. Though they stay away from populated areas, they are often found in the serene glades of Mount Hyjal.

Quillboars

Quillboars are a race of primitive boar-men that have razor sharp spines protruding from their muscular, hunched backs. These resilient, fearless creatures inhabit the central Barrens of Kalimdor in the labyrinthine maze of thorns called Razorfen Downs.

Sludge Beasts

These strange creatures share an elemental heritage, but have been corrupted by the powers of chaos. Now they exist as tortured masses of semi-sentient goo. No one knows what their motivations are or if there is any specific ecology behind their existence.

Spiders

Though many scholars believe that all spiders trace their roots back to the ancient kingdom of Azjol-Nerub, the giant spiders of Kalimdor have made a claim to the shadowy corners of Ashenvale Forest. Though not necessarily evil, wild spiders can become fearsome opponents if they feel their nests have been defiled.

Satyrs

Satyrs were once night elves who practiced the magical arts in the days before the War of the Ancients. These magically corrupted night elves, having given themselves over to the will of the Legion, became terribly cursed. Though they retained a portion of their magical power, their bodies were warped and twisted into those of beasts. Now the satyrs exist only to harry their hated night elf cousins and obey the will of the Legion – which they believe will one day return.

Vulture

These avian creatures are found throughout the Barrens – seeking carnage upon which to feed. The mottled scavengers have been known to aid the vile harpies from time to time – drawn by the promise of freshly slain flesh and blood.

Heroes and Villains

Antonidas

Occupation: Human Archmage - Head of the Kirin Tor of Dalaran
Affiliation: The Kirin Tor
Age: 71

Antonidas is the head of the Kirin Tor, the conclave of wizards that rules over the magical kingdom of Dalaran. This venerable Archmage is reputedly one of the most powerful wizards in the world. Though his failing health prohibits him from spending to much time away from his beloved city, his apprentice, Jaina Proudmoore, serves as his eyes and ears in the world. Antonidas looks forward to the day when he will hand his power and mantle of leadership over to Jaina, who he feels will make a most impressive Archmage.

Archimonde

Occupation: Eredar Overlord of the Legion Forces
Affiliation: The Burning Legion
Age: Unknown

Archimonde the Defiler was one of the first demons to rally behind Sargeras when the Burning Legion was formed. Archimonde is heartless and brutal, but very cunning and far sighted. The colossal demon wields limitless warlock magics and primal strength to lay waste to any who would oppose his fiery will. In his heart of hearts, he seeks to become a god and wield powers that rival those of Sargeras himself. After ten thousand years of waiting, he is prepared to invade the world of Azeroth once again. Though he is committed to carry out the invasion in Sargeras' name, he may have ulterior motives in mind for the world and its innate magics.

Cairne Bloodhoof

Occupation: Tauren Warrior - Chieftain of the Bloodhoof Tribe
Affiliation: The Horde
Age: 99

The mighty chief of the Bloodhoof tauren, Cairne is a peerless warrior and a wise leader of his ancient people. Though slowed somewhat by the weight of age, Cairne still possesses the strength and valor of twenty men. This greathearted giant knows that his people are in grave danger of extermination from the marauding centaurs. However, he has never given up hope of one day finding a way to lead his people to a new land where they can make their home and live in peace.

Grom Hellscream

Occupation: Orc Warrior - Chieftain of the Warsong Clan
Affiliation: The Horde
Age: 46

Grom Hellscream is the last surviving orc chieftain from Draenor. Having led his mighty Warsong clan to countless victories over the humans, Hellscream despaired at the lethargy that overcame his race after the Second War. Hellscream was one of the first orcs to fall victim to the demons' curse on his race. He has struggled with the rage and bloodlust within his heart for many long years. Now, under Thrall's visionary, idealistic leadership, Hellscream believes that he and his people can finally be freed from the demons' corrupting influence.

Illidan Stormrage

Occupation: Night Elf Demon Hunter - Former Sorcerer
Affiliation: None...
Age: 15,032

In the dark days, before the War of the Ancients, Illidan was one of the few non-high-borne practitioners of magic. Though his older brother, Furion, warned him that magic was an evil, corrupting power, Illidan steadfastly refused to give up his coveted art. Over time, the noble night Elf lost his soul to a dependency for magic's chaotic energies. Though Illidan used his dark powers to aid his brother against the demons of the Burning Legion, he ultimately betrayed his people by siding with the evil Queen Azshara and her followers. After the war ended and the landmass of Kalimdor was shattered forever, Illidan created a new Well of Eternity to ensure that his coveted, corrupting magic would not disappear from the world. For his sin, his brother, Furion, commanded that he be chained beneath the earth for all time. Illidan has remained caged in darkness ever since.

Jaina Proudmoore

Occupation: Human Sorceress - Special Agent of the Kirin Tor
Affiliation: The Alliance
Age: 23

Perhaps one of the most gifted sorceresses to train in Dalaran for generations, Jaina is a bright, inquisitive young woman who constantly strives to expand her powers and knowledge of magic. Her father, Admiral Proudmoore of Kul Tiras, was one of the great heroes of the Second War. Jaina feels constant pressure to live up to her father's name, but wishes only to study and follow her path of magical investigation. Like Arthas, Jaina was deeply hurt when her affair with the young Prince ended. However, she

never let her disappointment interfere with her studies or her rigorous investigations. Her mentor, the Archmage Antonidas, has claimed that she may become the greatest sorceress humanity has ever produced.

Kel'Thuzad

Occupation: Human Necromancer - Leader of the Cult of the Damned
Affiliation: The Scourge
Age: 58

Kel'Thuzad was one of the greatest Archmagi of Dalaran. He was one of the members of the Kirin Tor and a dear friend of the Archmage Antonidas. However, his lust to delve into the dark arts of necromancy made him an outcast amongst his fellow wizards. Heeding the call of the god-like Lich King, Kel'Thuzad traveled to Northrend and offered his soul to Ner'zhul. The Lich King commanded the dark wizard to create a cult that would facilitate the creation of a grand, undead army. Kel'Thuzad used his powers and vast fortune to found the Cult of the Damned – the sinister group that would bring Ner'zhul's dark will to fruition...

Mannoroth

Occupation: Demon King of the Pit Lords
Affiliation: The Burning Legion
Age: Unknown

Mannoroth the Destructor is a being of pure hate, malice, and rage. He is the ultimate living engine of destruction, seeking only to raze and murder everything in his path. It has been speculated that he has some significant ties to the orcish race – that he may be the original source of their bloodlust and corruption, but this has yet to be proven. Mannoroth has waited ten thousand years to return and finish the job he started during the War of the Ancients. Now, at last, his time for vengeance has come.

Malfurion Stormrage

Occupation: Night Elf Arch Druid
Affiliation: The Sentinels
Age: 15,032

Furion was the first night elf to oppose the evil Queen Azshara and her demon-worshiping high-borne. He, along with his brother Illidan and the demi-god Cenarius, led the battle against the Burning Legion during the War of the Ancients. He was the first to forsake magic and adopt the tenets of druidism. He has been the spiritual leader of the night elves for over ten thousand years and has worked to safeguard his people's fragile culture – even from within the trance-like state of the Emerald Dream.

Muradin Bronzebeard

Occupation: Dwarven Prospector - Former Ambassador of Ironforge
Affiliation: The Alliance, Explorer's Guild of Ironforge
Age: 221

Muradin is the brother of King Magni Bronzebeard of Ironforge. During the dark days of the Second War, Muradin served as the liaison between Lordaeron and the dwarves' realm of Khaz Modan. While at the court of Lordaeron, Muradin befriended the youthful Arthas and taught him how to master fighting blades of every type. Muradin was one of the first dwarves to establish the Explorer's Guild, a group dedicated to archaeology and exploration of the unknown world. Though Muradin rarely has a chance to visit Khaz Modan or Lordaeron anymore, he is a firm supporter of the dwarves' alliance with the humans.

Prince Arthas

Occupation: Human Paladin - Crown Prince of Lordaeron
Affiliation: The Alliance, Knights of the Silver Hand
Age: 24

The only son of King Terenas, Arthas is an idealistic, yet somewhat rash, young man who dreams of one day succeeding his father as King of Lordaeron. Arthas became an apprentice paladin at nineteen and has served as a favorite pupil of Uther the Lightbringer ever since. Though Arthas loves the kindly Uther as an uncle, he longs to take command of his own destiny and become a hero like those brave veterans who fought the orcs during the Second War.

Despite the heartache he felt when his brief affair with the sorceress Jaina Proudmoore came to an end, Arthas has remained remarkably committed to his roles as both the Prince of Lordaeron and as a holy paladin. He has a deep reverence for the holy Light and wants nothing more than to safeguard his beloved people from harm.

Thrall, Son of Durotan

Occupation: Orc Shaman - Warchief of the Horde
Affiliation: The Horde
Age: 24

Thrall is the only son of the orc chieftain, Durotan, who was killed by assassins during the First War. As an infant, Thrall was found by human soldiers and raised as a slave and gladiator. Educated and trained in the arts of war, Thrall yearned for freedom and a chance to know his own people. The inexperienced Thrall escaped from bondage and set off to find others of his kind.

Thrall found the lethargic orcs and vowed to free them from their imprisonment and their demon curse. Studying the orcs' ancient rites of shamanism, Thrall learned how to wield the fury of the storms and earth. He succeeded in rallying his people and freeing them from the

human internment camps. For his honor, optimism and courage, Thrall was unanimously elected to be the new warchief of the orcish horde.

Tichondrius

Occupation: Nathrezim Dreadlord
Affiliation: The Scourge, Burning Legion
Age: Unknown

Tichondrius the darkener is an insidious demonic Dreadlord who revels in shadow and suffering. Though he honors the wishes of his master, Kil'jaeden, he resents his duty to watch over and police the Lich King, Ner'zhul. He believes that the Lich King will ultimately betray the Legion and attempt to free himself from its power. Tichondrius is, above all, a very good soldier. Though his own desire for power and conquest is fierce, he carries out his duties with calculated precision and care.

Tyrande Whisperwind

Occupation: Night Elf Priestess of the Moon - Leader of the Sentinel.
Affiliation: The Sentinels
Age: 13,836

Tyrande is an ancient night elf princess and high priestess of the moon goddess, Elune. In ages past, she aided Furion and Illidan Stormrage in their battle to save Kalimdor from the Burning Legion. As well as being Elune's high priestess, she is the leader of the Sentinels a group of warrior women who have sworn to protect Kalimdor's shores while their male counterparts, the druids, sleep in the trance-like Emerald Dream. Tyrande is a fiery warrior and holds certain resentment for shouldering the defense of her land while the druids sleep. Her undying love for Furion Stormrage has given her strength and courage enough to face the centuries alone and uphold her sacred charge to defend Kalimdor from any threat.

Uther the Lightbringer

Occupation: Human Paladin - Leader of the Knights of the Silver Hand
Affiliation: The Alliance
Age: 64

Uther was the first of the paladins blessed by the Archbishop Faol, prior to the Second War. He is a weathered veteran, respected as one of the greatest warriors in human history. Though it has been many years since war endangered his beloved Lordaeron, Uther has never tired in his duty to protect his land from demi-human threats and social unrest. The great-hearted leader of the paladins is perhaps the greatest general the Alliance has ever known. Only his wish to see Arthas become worthy of his father's crown has kept him from retiring and taking his due rest.

SAMWISE
02

Appendix: World Editor

The Warcraft III World Editor allows the creation of campaign and multiplayer maps. This is the most complete design tool Blizzard Entertainment has ever released to the public. This editor is virtually unchanged from the editor the level designers used to create their maps.

If you were a user of Staredit, you will find many things in common between Staredit and the Warcraft III editor, but you will also find that many things are different. With the move to a three-dimensional rendering engine, many options and features have been added, such as terrain formation and deformation, unit scaling, and camera control. Many restrictions that hampered creativity in preceding editors have been done away with to allow you much more flexibility and control over how your map is presented, your games are played, and your in-game movies are rendered.

The World Editor team wishes you many hours of enjoyment with this new editor. We can't wait to see some great maps!

PLEASE NOTE: Blizzard Entertainment does not directly support the editor. Our Technical Support team will be unable to answer questions about editor functionality or help resolve problems you may experience while using the editor.

World Editor Features & Navigation

Navigating Your Map

There are many ways to navigate your map. You can move up and down or left and right by using the scrollbars or the arrow keys on your keyboard. You can also move around by right-clicking on your map and dragging. Alternatively, you can change positions by left-clicking the minimap and dragging.

Due to the three-dimensional nature of Warcraft III maps, you now have the option to zoom in on and rotate your map. You can zoom in or out by holding down the Shift key and right-clicking and dragging on your map. You can rotate your map by holding down the Ctrl key and right-clicking and dragging on your map. If you press the C key to lock the game camera, you can then use the game's conventions for zooming in and rotating.

Previewer

The previewer is the box on the left side of you screen that allows you to see each unit or doodad that you have selected before you place it on the map. You can rotate and zoom in or out relative to each unit or doodad by using the arrow buttons located underneath the previewer. You can also see each animation under the various lighting options available by clicking on the arrows next to the associated time of day.

Brush List

The brush list is an alternative to the palettes. However, it only allows you to select the terrain, units, and doodads associated with the tileset you chose when you first created the map.

Map Creation & Settings

Creating a New Map

You can create a new map by selecting the option New in the File menu. You will then be given several options from which to choose:

Width – Determine the length of your map along its X-axis.

Height – Determine the length of your map along its Y-axis.

Playable Area – This is the area of your map that is actually playable; the Width and Height numbers include area reserved for boundary.

Size Description – The relative size of your map. This can be tiny, small, medium, large.

Tileset – This field allows you to modify what your initial tileset will be when you create your map.

Initial Tile – This field tells you what tile will cover your map's terrain when you begin. The default tile can be changed by clicking on any tile in the tileset you have chosen as your initial tileset.

Initial Cliff Level – Set the starting level of your map's terrain. For example, if your map starts at cliff level 14 (the highest), the terrain cannot be raised any higher. If you start at cliff level 0, the terrain cannot be lowered.

Initial Water Level – The initial water level of your map. If a water level is selected, your map will start covered by that level of water. Use the three buttons below this heading to set the default water level to None, Shallow Water, or Deep Water.

Random height field – Checking this option automatically raises and lowers the terrain, creating an uneven surface on your map when you begin.

Melee Versus Non-melee

A melee map in Warcraft III is one where the only player-owned units you place are starting locations, and there are no custom triggers, sounds, or units. The techtree properties and upgrade properties of your map have not been altered; if they have, your map is a non-melee map. You can, however, place doodads and neutral units. You can tell immediately if your map is a melee map or not by checking the lower right of the status bar.

Pathable and Unbuildable

Two concepts that you must understand when making both campaign and melee maps are pathability and buildability.

Pathability refers to what areas units can move through and around. For instance, the Orc Hero Tauren Chieftain is a much larger unit than an Orc Peon and therefore requires more area than a Peon to move through and around objects and terrain. Peons can path through places that a Tauren Chieftain could not. You can see pathing by hitting the P key or by selecting Pathing from the View menu.

Buildability refers to where units and buildings can be placed. There are certain tiles where buildings may not be placed, such as rock tiles. However, other units may be placed there. For instance, an uprooted Night Elf building may be placed on a rock tileset, but a rooted Night Elf building cannot.

Adjusting Your Map Properties

Your map's properties can be displayed and modified by selecting any of the first four options under the Scenario menu: Map Description, Map Size and Camera Bounds, Loading Screen, and Prologue Screen.

Map Description

Name – Here you can name your map.

Suggested Players – List what types of games and configurations your map works best with (e.g., 2v2, 2v2v2v2).

Description – Here you can tell players what to expect from your map.

Author – Give your name or your handle.

Reset Description Defaults – This option resets all four text fields to their default status.

Map Options

Hide minimap in preview screens – This prevents players from looking at an open map in the preview screens. When this option is checked, the minimap cannot be seen when in chat or when it is selected to create a multiplayer or single-player game.

Masked areas are partially visible – Areas in which the player hasn't traveled will be somewhat translucent to that player, rather than completely opaque (Black Mask), though far darker than the Fog of War. This option is referred to as Dark Mask.

Show water waves on cliff shores – This option enables the display of waves where water meets sharply defined land.

Show water waves on rolling shores – This option enables the display of waves where water meets smoothly sloping land.

Map Size and Camera Bounds

This section allows you to alter your map's size and camera bounds. In the center of the dialog box you will see a minimap. The sets of arrows that surround the minimap alter the map from the side they are on. The numbers next to each arrow under the headings Camera and Map denote the size of your map's viewable area and the total size of your map in small grid squares.

The two checkboxes, Modify Map Bounds and Modify Camera Bounds, let you modify the total size of your map and the size of your map's viewable area, respectively. If neither box is checked, you cannot click on any of the arrows. If only one option is checked, then you will only modify that.

The two statistics to the right of the checkboxes, Playable and Full, give the playable area of your map and the actual size of your map in medium grid squares.

Loading Screen

Use Default Screen – Use the default "Melee" loading screen.

Use Campaign Screen – Use a campaign screen you have chosen for your loading screen. Selecting this option will also make the following fields available: Loading Screen Title, Loading Screen Subtitle, and Loading Screen Text.

Loading Screen Title – The title displayed on your loading screen.

Loading Screen Subtitle – The subtitle displayed on your loading screen.

Loading Screen Text – Area for adding more text describing your map.

Prologue Screen

Use Default Screen – Use the default "Melee" prologue screen

Use Campaign Screen – Use a campaign screen you have chosen for your prologue screen. Selecting this option will also make the following fields available: Prologue Screen Title, Prologue Screen Subtitle, and Prologue Screen Text.

Prologue Screen Title – The title displayed on your prologue screen.

Prologue Screen Subtitle – The subtitle displayed on your prologue screen.

Prologue Screen Text – Area for adding more text describing your map.

Player Properties

Player Name – Here you can set player names.

Color – This is each player's color; these colors cannot be modified or reassigned.

Race – Choose the race of each player.

Controller – This option lets you set whether a player is computer controlled, user controlled, neutral, or rescuable.

Fixed Start Location – This option forces the editor to give a player a certain starting location.

Ally Priorities Properties

This section allows you to modify the precedence with which the game sets who will start at what starting location. It allows you to place teams together. The Low Priority category is evaluated after the High Priority category, but before the None category. To modify them, first check the box Modify Ally Priorities.

Force Properties

A force is similar to a team. You can put several players on the same force and make them start allied, with allied victory on, and even make the players share vision. To modify your player's forces, first check the box Use Custom Priorities. You can make people on a force have the following designations: Allied, Allied Victory, Share Vision, Share Unit Control, and Share Adv. Unit Control.

Techtree Properties

This section allows you modify what players can build what units. If there is a check next to a unit's name under the heading Available, that unit can be built. If the checkbox is empty, that unit cannot be constructed or trained. To do this you must first check the Use Custom Techtree box. (Please note that modifying this checkbox makes your map a non-melee map.)

Ability Properties

This allows you to prevent a player or players from using certain individual skills. For instance, you can allow a player to build Sorceresses, but then disallow the skills Slow, Invisibility, or Polymorph. To do this, you must check the Use Custom Abilities box. (Please note that modifying this checkbox makes your map a non-melee map.)

Upgrade Properties

This section allows you to decide the state of a player's research when he begins the game. If an upgrade is listed as Researched, then that player will start the game with that upgrade already researched. If an upgrade is listed as Unavailable, it cannot be researched. If it is Available, it can be researched. To do this you must first check the Use Custom Upgrades box. (Please note that modifying this checkbox makes your map a non-melee map.)

The Terrain Editor

The Terrain Editor is the main module of the World Editor. Here you can design and modify your terrain, as well as place units and doodads.

The Terrain Palette

To modify terrain, open your Terrain Palette by hitting the T key or by using the Window menu and choosing New Palette, then Terrain. Once the Terrain Palette opens, you have four categories of tools you can use.

The first section on the Terrain Palette is the Apply Texture section. By clicking on any of the tiles, you can select that tile and place it on your map. You may even place blight and boundary textures. Boundary is a special tile over which no unit can cross. It is similar in function to the blackness that surrounds your map. Blight is the disease that spreads over the ground near Undead buildings. The option Place Random Variation (on the previewer) allows the editor to place a random tile variation from the currently selected tile type, rather than placing only the tile variation you can see in the previewer.

Second is the Apply Cliff section. This section allows you to add and remove cliffs, shallow water, deep water, and ramps. You can also change what cliff you are using. You may increase or decrease the area modified by changing brush size.

The third section, the Apply Height section, has the following options:

Round – This tool allows you to make rounded hills. Holding down shift and left-clicking with this tool enabled allows you to create rounded valleys.

Plateau – This tool allows you to create perfectly flat surfaces on rounded hills and rounded valleys.

Noise – This tool creates an uneven, broken surface.

Smooth – This tool allows you to smooth out uneven surfaces.

The final section displays what brush shape and size you have selected and allows you to change these settings.

Modifying your Tileset

You can modify the tileset you have chosen or even create a custom tileset by selecting the option Modify Tileset under the Tools menu.

The Unit Palette

To place units on your map, simply open a Unit Palette by hitting the U key, or if you have a palette open, you can change that palette to the Unit Palette by left-clicking the down arrow and choosing Unit Palette.

The first menu specific to the Unit Palette is the list of possible unit owners:

Player X – This is a list of Players 1, 2, and so forth up to the maximum number of players you have allowed in your map via Player Properties.

Neutral Hostile – A contradiction in terms? Well, neutral hostile units don't care what player you are. They are hostile to all players, including computer-controlled players, but they are not hostile to other neutral hostile units.

Neutral Passive – These are units that will not attack even if attacked. Player units will not attack them unless ordered to; some neutral passive units (like the Goblin Merchant) cannot be attacked at all.

Items – Here you can select items to be placed directly on your map. This is not the place to decide what items your creeps will drop, though; for that, you need the Unit Properties dialog box, which you get by double-clicking a unit you've already placed on the map.

The second menu is the race menu. It allows you to place units of any race, even units that are outside the current player's race, including neutral hostile and neutral passive units.

The third section is where you find the units.

Player units (Orc, Human, Night Elf, and Undead) are divided into five categories.

Units – These are the non-Hero units available to a race. You will notice that there seem to be two of some units, like the Undead Gargoyle. This unit has two forms; thus, you have two options to place: a Gargoyle in regular form and a Gargoyle in Stone Form.

Heroes – These are the Heroes available to a race.

Buildings – This is a list of all the buildings each race can construct, including player starting locations. Only the rooted versions of Night Elf buildings will fall under this category if the currently selected race is Night Elf.

Uprooted Buildings – This section is specific to the certain races; it includes the uprooted form of all of the selected race's buildings that can be uprooted and moved.

Special – These are the units created specifically for campaigns.

Custom – This category only appears if you have created custom units in the Unit Editor.

In addition to the aforementioned categories, the neutral units also have two more categories. These units are further divided into groups based on tileset and level.

Unit Properties

After placing a unit, you can further modify it. To do this, double-click a unit you have placed, or select the unit and choose Edit Properties in the Edit menu.

The Doodad Palette

To place doodads, open the Doodad Palette by hitting the D key or by selecting Doodads from the Layer menu. Doodads are generally non-interactive objects placed on a map for visual appeal. The big exception is the tree doodad; trees are consumable.

Doodads are organized by tileset and by category. The doodad categories are the same for every tileset, but not every tileset has doodads that fall into each category.

Next there are several buttons on the Doodad Palette:

Random Rotation – When this button is pressed, it changes the doodad to face a random direction when placed.

Random Scale – When this button is pressed, the placed doodad will be of a random size.

Place Random Variation – Most doodads will have at least one other variation; with this option selected, the editor will randomly select a variation to be placed.

The last two things on the menu are the list of available doodads and the brush menu.

Doodad Properties

After placing a doodad you can further modify it just like a unit. To do this, double-click on a placed doodad or select Edit Properties from the Edit menu. You have the following options, though not all are available for every doodad.

Variation – Some doodads have multiple variations on the same model, you can select a new variation here.

Rotation – Some doodads can face many multiple directions, though others are quite limited.

Scale (%) – You can modify the scale of the doodad along each vertex (x, y, z) by manipulating the various numbers next to each vertex. Not all doodads can be manipulated in all vertices however.

Life (%) – You can modify the starting life of destructible doodads. Even setting them to zero.

The Camera Palette

The Camera Palette can be found by hitting the M key or by selecting Cameras from the Layer menu. This palette is designed to complement a trigger that uses it. If you don't specify triggers in your script to see the action through your cameras, then the player will never know they exist.

The Region Palette

Regions, like cameras, need triggers to reference them so that they can be properly used. Otherwise, they will have no effect in the game. They can be used to set off triggers or to delineate areas a trigger will affect. This aspect will be explained in more detail when we discuss the Trigger Editor. There are exceptions to this rule of linking regions with triggers, and they involve weather effects, Way Gates, and ambient sounds.

The Region Palette is relatively simple. Clicking on Add will allow you to add a region. The white field below these two buttons contains a list of all the currently placed regions. If you right-click a listed region, you can edit its properties, view it, and delete it.

Region Properties

This dialog box can be reached by double-clicking on a region in the Terrain Editor or by right-clicking on a region in the Region Palette and selecting Edit Properties. This dialog box has the following options:

The first field allows you to modify your region's name. If you change this field, it will also change the variable name of your region. The variable name is gg_rct_Region_XXX, located underneath the modifiable name field.

The four numeric fields below the region's name field allow you to modify the size of the region by adjusting each of the region's four sides.

The Weather Effect checkbox allows you to add weather effects through regions. This is the only method available to designers who wish to have weather effects on melee maps. Otherwise triggers must be used, and the map will become a non-melee map.

The Ambient Sound checkbox allows you to add ambient sounds that will play in specified regions.

Way Gates

Way Gates are a special neutral passive unit in the game used in combination with regions. If you place a Way Gate and then open its Unit Properties dialog, you can make that Way Gate transport units to any region on the map by putting a check in the box Way Gate Active and then selecting a destination.

The Sound Editor

The Sound Editor allows you to import and export sound (.wav) files and music (.mp3) files, and then play these sounds through triggers in the Trigger Editor. To open the Sound Editor, use F5 or choose Sound Editor from the Module menu.

The Unit Editor

This is another powerful addition to the World Editor, and it is recommended that you become familiar with the game before you use it, lest you delve too deeply into the inner workings of the game too quickly. To open the Unit Editor, use F6, or choose Unit Editor from the Module window.

The Object manager

Because there are so many objects and ways in which they can be linked in this powerful new editor, there must be an efficient and easy way of managing them; hence, the need for the Object Manager.

Credits

Game Design
Blizzard Entertainment

Executive Producer
Mike Morhaime

Team Lead
Frank Pearce

Art Director
Samwise Didier

Lead Designer
Rob Pardo

Lead Technical Artist
Rob McNaughton

Producer
Chris Sigaty

Technology Lead
Jay Patel

Programming
Andy Bond, Carl Chimes, Jeff Chow, Alan Dabiri, Bob Fitch, Monte Krol, Dave Lawrence, Graham Madarasz, Collin Murray, Jay Patel, Frank Pearce, Andrea Pessino, Brett Wood

Additional Programming
Mike Heiberg, Sam Lantinga, Mike Morhaime, John Stiles, Tim Truesdale, Matthew Versluys, Jeremy Wood

Battle.net Programming
James Anhalt, Robert Bridenbecker, Brian Fitzgerald, Tony Tribelli, Matthew Versluys

Macintosh Programming
John Stiles

Additional Macintosh Programming
Rob Barris, John Mikros, Brett Wood

Artists
Dave Berggren, Samwise Didier, Allen Dilling, Trevor Jacobs, Roman Kenney, Rob McNaughton, Micky Neilson, Matt Oursbourn, Ted Park, Stu Rose, Ru Weerasuriya

Additional Art
Kevin Beardslee, Adam Byrne, Brandon Idol, Kyle Harrison, Eric Henze, Solomon Lee, Justin Thavirat

Senior Designer
Allen Adham

Writer & Creative Director
Chris Metzen

Campaign Design & Layout
Tim Campbell, David Fried, Dave Hale, Michael Heiberg, Scott Mercer, Matt Morris, Rob Pardo, Dean Shipley

Story Concept
Samwise Didier, Chris Metzen, Rob Pardo

Script & Text Editing
Micky Neilson, Susan Sams, Ru Weerasuriya

Associate Producers
Frank Gilson, Chris Millar

Cinematic Director
Nicholas S. Carpenter

Cinematic Executive Producer
Matt Samia

Cinematic Producer
Scott Abeyta

Cinematic Editor
Joeyray Hall

Cinematic Script Writers
Nicholas S. Carpenter, Chris Metzen

Cinematic Artists
Scott Abeyta, John Burnett, Nicholas S. Carpenter, John Chalfant, Jeff Chamberlain, Aaron Chan, Ben Dai, Joe Frayne, Jay Hathaway, Harley D. Huggins II, Jared Keller, Jon Lanz, James McCoy, Matthew Mead, Dennis Price, Matt Samia, Mark Skelton, Patrick Thomas, Seth Thompson, Ru Weerasuriya, Kenson Yu

Cinematic Technical Artists & Tools Development
Scott Abeyta, John Burnett, Jeff Chamberlain, Aaron Chan, Joe Frayne, Steeg Haskell, Jared Keller, Jon Lanz, Alen Lapidis

Additional Cinematic Work
Dan Burke, Paul Hormis, Brit Snyder, Thayrn Valavanis

Audio Director
Glenn Stafford

Music
Tracy W. Bush, Derek Duke, Jason Hayes, Glenn Stafford

Sound Design
Tracy W. Bush, Tami Donner Harrison, Derek Duke, Brian Farr, Glenn Stafford

Voice Direction & Internal Casting
Tracy W. Bush, Nichoals S. Carpenter, Tami Donner Harrison, Jason Hayes, Chris Metzen, Micky Neilson

Voice Editing
Tami Donner Harrison

Outside Voice Casting by
Donald Paul Pemrick, Dean E. Fronk

Outside Voice Casting Assistants
Amanda Fenster, Gerg Sacks

Voice Acting
Michael Barken, Richard Barnes, Michael Bradberry, Fredrick Bloggs, Tracy W. Bush, Piera Coppola, Jackson Daniels, Samwise Didier, Tami Donner Harrison, Derek Duke, Alex Dumas, Richard George, Carrie Gordon Lowrey, Michael McConnohie, Michael Gough, Justin Gross, Tiffany Hayes, Thomas Jung, Matthew King, Monte Krol, Abe Lasser, Rob McNaughton, Chris Metzen, Lani Minella, Calab Moody, Bob Papenbrook, Gary Platner, Bill Roper, Glenn Stafford, Kai Vilhelmsen, Ted Whitney

Additional Game Review
Allen Adham, Chris Arretche, Dave Brevik, Samwise Didier, Eric Dodds, Bob Fitch, Geoff Fraizer, Mike Morhaime, Bill Roper, Max Schaefer, Tyler Thompson, Ian Welke

Manual Development and Editing
Eli Catalan, Elliott Chin, Melissa Edwards, Jason Hutchins, Scott Mercer, Chris Metzen, Susan Sams, Mikey Schaefer, EvelynSmith, Peter Underwood

Manual Artwork
Chris Metzen, Ted Park, Ru Weerasuriya Samwise Didier, Justin Thavirat

Quality Assurance Management
Christopher Manley, Mark Moser, Ian Welke

QA Lead Tester
Ed Kang

QA Assistant Lead Tester
Kelly Chun

QA Technical Engineer
Evelyn Smith

QA Team Leads
Zach Allen, Michael Backus, Ilya Berelson, Zach Callanan, Michael Chu, Les Douglas, Robert Foote, Ron Frybarger, Gary Gibson, Manny Gonzales, Ray Labauch, Dean Lee, Matt Lee, Brian Love, Jonathan Mankin, Sean McCrea, Michael Murphy, Justin Parker, Dean Shimonishi, Stan Wang

Game Testers
Aaron Adams, Michael Barken, Andrew Brownell, Edward Bui, Jeremy Cargilo, Shane Cargilo, Charles Carter, James Chadwick, Bryan Chen, Jack Chen, Michelle Elbert, Jason Fader, Christopher Fisher, Arthur Fong, Derek Johnstone, Dennis Lam, Jonas Laster, Nicholas Lawson, Allen Lin, John Meyers, Kaeo Milker, Brian Mitchell, Danny Nguyen, Nick Pisani, William Roseman, Michael Schaefer, Emilio Segura, Lloyd Tullues, Brian Urquhart, John Wick, Stephen Wong, John Yoo

Additional Testers
Ted Barken, Jeanette Clausen, David Dooley, Tod Fay, Josh Hillborn, Jeff Mclean, Samuel Schrimsher, Eric Strauss, Cosmo Taormina

Technical Support Management
Thor Biafore, John Schwartz

Online Support
Timothy Fox, Edward Hanes, Mike Kramer, Alen Lapidis, David Nguyen, Michael Nguyen, Collin Smith, Martin Tande, Kenny Zigler

Technical Support
Geoff Goodman, Norman Harms, John Hsieh, Kris Nedrebo, Richard Sanford, Adam Slack, Jason Stilwell

Localization & Macintosh Producer
Jason Hutchins

Globalization Producer
Flavie Gufflet

Localization Project Manager
Barry Kehoe

Localization Project Leads
Caitriona Finlay, David Hickey, Padraig McCaul

Localization Lead Engineer
Damien Monaghan

Localization Engineers
Attila Edelenyi, Jason King, Monte Krol, Brendan O' Mahony, Stuart Nolan

Localization QA Leads
Jesus Baquedano Ferrer, David Hickey

Localization QA
Francis" Frux" Courchinoux, Nelly Dietrich, Andrew Hagger, Franchesco Musso, J.C. Pastor "pAsh"

International Web Teams
Sebastien Gernault, Steve Martin, Georges Martins, Stefanie Pranz, Myriam Santoso

Business Development
Paul W. Sams

Additional Business Development & Operations
Elaine DiIorio, Melissa Edwards, Isaac Matarasso

Battle.net Producer
John Lagrave

Battle.net Network Engineers
Adrian Luff, Hung Nguyen

Information Technologies
Mike Hale, Kris Mackey, Kirk Mahony, Isaac Matarasso, Hung Nguyen, Jeremy Smith, Robert Van Dusen

Office Administration
Christina Cade, Jamie Neveaux, Lisa Schoner

Financial Management
David Gee, Paul W. Sams

Public Relations
Lisa Bucek, Susan Sams, Gil Shif, Beau Yarbrough

Web Team
Elaine DiIorio, Geoff Fraizer, Mike Hein, Ted Park, Blaine Whittle

Legal Counsel
Kevin Crook, Will Glenn (in loving memory), Bob Marafioti, Rob Rigole, Eric Roeder, Patrick Sweeney

Global Brand Management
Neal Hubbard, Stewart Weiss

Marketing & Creative Services
Kathy Carter, Jessica Drossin, Elisabeth Miller, Steven Parker, Hayley Sumner, Bill Watt

Packaging Artwork
Justin Thavirat

North American Sales
Philip O'Neil, Bruce Slywka

International Sales, Marketing, & PR
Chris Ansell, Michael Fuller, Hubert Larenaudie, Cyril Marchal, Cedric Marechal, Christophe Ramboz, Stephane Vallet, Mark Warburton, Kim Watt

Direct Sales
Rob Beatie, Kim Bridenbecker

Manufacturing
Tom Bryan, Jaime Chavez, Bob Wharton

Recruiting
Pat Nagle, Derek Simmons, Jack Sterling, Bernie Wilkins

Global Launch Team
Lisa Bucek, Gerry Carty, Melissa Edwards, Lang Fredrickson, Michael Fuller, Flavie Gufflet, Neal Hubbard, Jason Hutchins, Hubert Larenaudie, Cyril Marchal, Cedric Marechal, Mike Morhaime, Philip O'Neil, Christophe Ramboz, Paul W. Sams, Chris Sigaty, Bruce Slywka, Luc Vanhal, Steve Voorma, Mark Warburton, Bob Wharton, Edward Zinser

Battle.net Hosting Partners
AT&T, DACOM, Telia

Dunsel Specialist
Shane Dabiri

Thanks To
Jean-Marie Messier, Eric Licoys, Agnes Touraine, Ken Cron, Edwards Zinser, Jay Meschel, Sandy Gunn, Cameron Buschardt, The Warcraft III Beta Testers, Adrian Bourke, John Funnell, Darrius Thompson, Bart Farkas, Wade Farrell, Mike O'Brien, Jeff Strain, Pat Wyatt, Paula Duffy, Danny Kearns, Todd Coyle, Ralph Becker, Mark Kern, Eric Schaefer, Scott Boness, Edwin Braun, Ray "Gramps" Chamberlain, Keith Galocy, Lin Kayser, Ivan Kolev, Amir Sinanovic, Shawn Steiner, Kresimir Tkalcec, Scott Petersen, Liam Byrne, Jack Buser, Charlie Brissette, Dave Philipson, Dr. Fred Siciliano,

Special Thanks
Blizzard North, Luc Vanhal, Bob & Jan Davidson

We want to extend a very special thanks to all our families. Your never-ending patience and understanding made it all possible. We love you!

Additional Thanks

Celeste Aviva, Ian & Rosemary Gilson, Ronald J. Millar Sr., Susan Krol, Garrett & Tori Fitch, House Madarasz, The Sigaty Family, Jamie Neveaux, Lisa Pearce, Raf Cecco, Xabier Abaroa, The Bond Family, Diana Smallwood, Pamina Elgueta, Tiffany Neilson, Carin & Madisyn Jacobs, Amy Dilling, Christy Goddess, Tracy Park, Tracey "Minxey" McNaughton, Alicia Campbell, Maye McGowan-Hale, Jennifer Deem, April Palmer, Walt Simonson, Sydney Pardo, The Heiberg Family, Nikita Mikros, Petros Melissakis, William Hutchins, Karen Barris, Jon Ritman, Walter Takata, Pamela & Traver Campbell, Hector Fried, Ghost Platoon (Black Sheep), Strada, Donik the Irritable Narwhal, E:OS, Rush, Legacy of Steel, ME, Shaq, Inner Loop, Tenacious D, John Carpenter, Ripper Owens, Shmoo, The Parasite, Ferrari, Porsche, Mucho Hot Chicken, Bruce Lee, Samurai Showdown II, Thursday Karaoke Nights, Ray the Soda Guy, Hilda's Catering, Simba, Edwin Braun, John and Gai Burnett, Daisy Campbell, Lisa Carden, Jo Anne, David, and Jason Carpenter, Brad Chamberlain, Laura Clifton, Stacy Frayne, the Griffith Clan, Jason and Damian Hall, the Henderson Clan, Melissa "Chagirl" Huggins, Peter Jackson, Barbara and Tilden Keller, Debbie Lanz, Henry Luvert, the McCoy Clan, Shelly "Saucy" Mead, Mummsy Mead, Judah Mehler, Sheryl Narahara, Don and Becky Price, Amma and Thaththa Ru, Stephanie, Ryan, David, and Christopher Samia, Elizabeth and Jessica Skelton, Tara and Jacob Thomas, Randal and Debra Thompson, Sin Li, Wai Kien, and Kerwin Yu, Susan, Ethan, Quinn and Aaron Stafford, Kyle Harrison, Tracy Farr, Tiffany Hayes, Alison and Madeline Jane Bush, Susan, Matthew, and Michael Sams, Megan Wooley, Rich Hernandez, Blizzard Hockey, Snuzzle, Eliot Kang, Juba, Steve and Vicky Oglesby, Jim and Kay Sams, Gayle Dunseth, Lisalee, The Gibson Family, Eltha Dee, Dominique Chang, Paul Mankin, Jennifer Ongun, Andy Ongun, Titanium Wang, Vanadium Wang, Clarinda Allen, Peter Gates, Christina Sprague, Sofia Vergara, Lisa Boyle, Comic Quest, The Rally Monkey, Mitsuwa Marketplace, Brenda McCrea, Brandee, ReneE Kushnir, Josh Honeyman, Holly Matecki.

YOU SHOULD CAREFULLY READ THE FOLLOWING END USER LICENSE AGREEMENT BEFORE INSTALLING THIS SOFTWARE PROGRAM. BY INSTALLING, COPYING, OR OTHERWISE USING THE SOFTWARE PROGRAM, YOU AGREE TO BE BOUND BY THE TERMS OF THIS AGREEMENT. IF YOU DO NOT AGREE TO THE TERMS OF THIS AGREEMENT, PROMPTLY RETURN THE UNUSED SOFTWARE PROGRAM TO THE PLACE OF PURCHASE OR CONTACT BLIZZARD ENTERTAINMENT CUSTOMER SERVICE AT (949) 955-1382 FOR A FULL REFUND OF THE PURCHASE PRICE WITHIN 30 DAYS OF THE ORIGINAL PURCHASE.

This software program including any and all subsequent patches (the "Program"), any printed materials, any on-line or electronic documentation, and any and all copies and derivative works of such software program and materials are the copyrighted work of Blizzard Entertainment, a division of Vivendi Universal Games, Inc. and/or it wholly owned subsidiaries, or its suppliers. All use of the Program is governed by the terms of the End User License Agreement which is provided below ("License Agreement"). The Program is solely for use by end users according to the terms of the License Agreement. Any use, reproduction, or redistribution of the Program not in accordance with the terms of the License Agreement is expressly prohibited.

END USER LICENSE AGREEMENT

1. Limited Use License. Blizzard Entertainment ("Blizzard") hereby grants, and by installing the Program you thereby accept, a limited, non-exclusive license and right to install and use one (1) copy of the Program for your use on a home, business, or portable computer. The Program also contains a 'World Editor' (the "Editor") that allows you to create custom levels or other materials for your personal use in connection with the Program ("New Materials"). All use of the Editor or any New Materials is subject to this License Agreement. In addition, the Program has a multiplayer capability that allows users to utilize the Program over the Internet exclusively via Blizzard Entertainment's online game network Battle.net or other hosting service authorized by Blizzard Entertainment. Use of the Program over Battle.net or other hosting service authorized by Blizzard Entertainment is subject to your acceptance of Battle.net's Terms of Use Agreement. Blizzard Entertainment reserves the right to update, modify or change the Battle.net Terms of Use Agreement at any time.

2. Ownership. All title, ownership rights, and intellectual property rights in and to the Program and any and all copies thereof (including, but not limited to, any titles, computer code, themes, objects, characters, character names, stories, dialog, catch phrases, locations, concepts, artwork, animations, sounds, musical compositions, audio-visual effects, methods of operation, moral rights, any related documentation, and "applets" incorporated into the Program) are owned by Blizzard Entertainment or its licensors. The Program is protected by the copyright laws of the United States, international copyright treaties, and conventions and other laws. All rights are reserved. The Program contains certain licensed materials, and Blizzard's licensors may protect their rights in the event of any violation of this Agreement.

3. Responsibilities of End User.

A. Subject to the Grant of License hereinabove, you may not, in whole or in part, copy, photocopy, reproduce, sublicense, translate, reverse engineer, derive source code, modify, disassemble, decompile, create a source code equivalent, create derivative works based on the Program, or remove any proprietary notices or labels on the Program, or allow others to do so, without the prior consent, in writing, of Blizzard.

B. The Program is licensed to you as a single product. Its component parts may not be separated for use on more than one computer.

C. You are entitled to use the Program for your own use, but you are not entitled to:

(i) sell, grant a security interest in, or transfer reproductions of the Program to other parties in any way, nor to rent, lease, or license the Program to others without the prior written consent of Blizzard;

(ii) exploit the Program or any of its parts for any commercial purpose including, but not limited to, use at a cyber café, computer gaming center, or any other location-based site. Blizzard may offer a separate Site License Agreement to permit you to make the Program available for commercial use; contact Blizzard for details;

(iii) use or allow third parties to use the Editor and the New Materials created thereby for commercial purposes including, but not limited to, distribution of New Materials on a stand-alone basis or packaged with other software or hardware through any and all distribution channels, including, but not limited to, retail sales and on-line electronic distribution without the express written consent of Blizzard;

(iv) host or provide matchmaking services for the Program, or emulate or redirect the communication protocols used by Blizzard in the network feature of the Program, through protocol emulation, tunneling, modifying or adding components to the Program, use of a utility program, or any other techniques now known or hereafter developed, for any purpose including, but not limited to, network play over the Internet, network play utilizing commercial or non-commercial gaming networks, or as part of content aggregation networks without the prior written consent of Blizzard; and

(v) create or maintain, under any circumstance, more than one simultaneous connection to Battle.net or other hosting services authorized by Blizzard Entertainment. All such connections to Battle.net or other hosting services authorized by Blizzard Entertainment, whether created by the Program or by other tools and utilities, may only be made through methods and means expressly approved by Blizzard Entertainment. Under no circumstances may you connect, or create tools that allow you to connect to Battle.net's private binary interface or interfaces other than those explicitly provided by Blizzard Entertainment for public use.

4. Program Transfer. You may permanently transfer all of your rights under this License Agreement, provided the recipient agrees to the terms of this License Agreement and you agree to remove the Program and any New Materials from your home, business, or portable computer.

5. Termination. This License Agreement is effective until terminated. You may terminate the License Agreement at any time by destroying the Program and any New Materials. Blizzard may, at its discretion, terminate this License Agreement in the event that you fail to comply with the terms and conditions contained herein. In such event, you must immediately destroy the Program and any New Materials.

6. Export Controls. The Program may not be re-exported, downloaded, or otherwise exported into (or to a national or resident of) any country to which the U.S. has embargoed goods, or to anyone on the U.S. Treasury Department's list of Specially Designated Nationals or the U.S. Commerce Department's Table of Denial Orders. By installing the Program, you are agreeing to the foregoing, and you are representing and warranting that you are not located in, under the control of, or a national or resident of any such country or on any such list.

7. Customer Service/Technical Support. Blizzard agrees to provide Customer Service and Technical Support for this Program until such time as the Program is "Out of Publication." The Program shall be considered "Out of Publication" one (1) year following the date that the Program is no longer manufactured and/or distributed by Blizzard, or its licensors. "Customer Service" as used herein may be provided to you by Blizzard representatives by telephone and/or by electronic message (e-mail). "Technical Support" may be provided to you by Blizzard by telephone, electronic message (e-mail), or by posting of information related to known technical support issues on a web site. Unless otherwise stated in the Program's packaging or in the Program's user manual, nothing herein shall be construed so as to place a duty upon Blizzard to provide Customer Service or Technical Support via a toll-free telephone number for an unlimited period of time.

8. Duration of the "On-Line" component of the Program. This Program contains an 'on-line' component that allows you to utilize the Product over the Internet utilizing servers and software maintained or authorized by Blizzard. Blizzard agrees to provide the servers and software technology necessary to utilize the "on-line" component of the Program until such time as the Program is Out of Publication, as defined above. Thereafter, Blizzard may, in its sole discretion, continue to provide the servers and software technology necessary to utilize the "on-line" component of the Program, or Blizzard may license to third parties the right to provide the servers and software technology necessary to utilize the "on-line" component of this Program. However, nothing contained herein shall be construed so as to place an obligation upon Blizzard to provide the servers and software technology necessary to utilize the "on-line" beyond the time that the Program is Out of Publication.

9. Limited Warranty. Blizzard expressly disclaims any warranty for the Program, Editor, and Manual(s). The Program, Editor, and Manual(s) are provided "as is" without warranty of any kind, either express or implied, including, without limitation, the implied warranties of merchantability, fitness for a particular purpose, or noninfringement. The entire risk arising out of use or performance of the Program, Editor, and Manual(s) remains with the User; however Blizzard warrants up to and including ninety (90) days from the date of your purchase of the Program that the media containing the Program shall be free from defects in material and workmanship. In the event that the media proves to be defective during that time period, and upon presentation to

Blizzard of proof of purchase of the defective Program, Blizzard will at its option 1) correct any defect, 2) provide you with a product of equal or lesser value, or 3) refund your money. Some states do not allow the exclusion or limitation of implied warranties or liability for incidental damages, so the above limitations may not apply to you.

10. Limitation of Liability. NEITHER BLIZZARD, VIVENDI UNIVERSAL GAMES, INC., ITS PARENT, SUBSIDIARIES, OR AFFILIATES SHALL BE LIABLE IN ANY WAY FOR LOSS OR DAMAGE OF ANY KIND RESULTING FROM THE USE OF THE PROGRAM, THE EDITOR, OR BLIZZARD ENTERTAINMENT'S ONLINE GAME NETWORK, BATTLE.NET, OR OTHER ON-LINE PROVIDER AUTHORIZED BY BLIZZARD ENTERTAINMENT, INCLUDING, BUT NOT LIMITED TO, LOSS OF GOODWILL, WORK STOPPAGE, COMPUTER FAILURE OR MALFUNCTION, OR ANY AND ALL OTHER COMMERCIAL DAMAGES OR LOSSES. ANY WARRANTY AGAINST INFRINGEMENT THAT MAY BE PROVIDED IN SECTION 2-312(3) OF THE UNIFORM COMMERCIAL CODE AND/OR IN ANY OTHER COMPARABLE STATE STATUTE IS EXPRESSLY DISCLAIMED. FURTHER, BLIZZARD ENTERTAINMENT SHALL NOT BE LIABLE IN ANY WAY FOR THE LOSS OR DAMAGE TO ACCOUNTS (INCLUDING BUT NOT LIMITED TO PLAYER CHARACTERS OR ITEMS), STATISTICS, OR USER PROFILE INFORMATION STORED ON BATTLE.NET OR OTHER ON-LINE PROVIDER AUTHORIZED BY BLIZZARD ENTERTAINMENT. BLIZZARD ENTERTAINMENT SHALL NOT BE RESPONSIBLE FOR ANY INTERRUPTIONS OF SERVICE ON BATTLE.NET OR OTHER ON-LINE PROVIDER AUTHORIZED BY BLIZZARD ENTERTAINMENT INCLUDING, BUT NOT LIMITED TO, ISP DISRUPTIONS, SOFTWARE OR HARDWARE FAILURES, OR ANY OTHER EVENT WHICH MAY RESULT IN A LOSS OF DATA OR DISRUPTION OF SERVICE. Some states do not allow the exclusion or limitation of incidental or consequential damages, or allow limitations on how long an implied warranty lasts, so the above limitations may not apply.

11. Equitable Remedies. You hereby agree that Blizzard would be irreparably damaged if the terms of this License Agreement were not specifically enforced, and therefore you agree that Blizzard shall be entitled, without bond, other security, or proof of damages, to appropriate equitable remedies with respect to breaches of this License Agreement, in addition to such other remedies as Blizzard may otherwise have available to it under applicable laws. In the event any litigation is brought by either party in connection with this License Agreement, the prevailing party, in such litigation shall be entitled to recover from the other party all the costs, attorneys' fees and other expenses incurred by such prevailing party in the litigation.

12. Limitations on License. Nothing in this License Agreement shall preclude you from making or authorizing the making of another copy or adaptation of the Program provided, however, that (1) such new copy or adaptation is created as an essential step in your utilization of the Program in accordance with the terms of this License Agreement and for NO OTHER PURPOSE; or (2) such new copy or adaptation is for archival purposes ONLY and all archival copies are destroyed in the event of your Transfer of the Program, the Termination of this Agreement, or other circumstances under which your continued use of the Program ceases to be rightful.

13. Miscellaneous. This License Agreement shall be deemed to have been made and executed in the State of California, and any dispute arising hereunder shall be resolved in accordance with the law of California. You agree that any claim asserted in any legal proceeding by one of the parties against the other shall be commenced and maintained in any state or federal court located in the State of California, County of Los Angeles, having subject matter jurisdiction with respect to the dispute between the parties. This License Agreement may be amended, altered, or modified only by an instrument in writing, specifying such amendment, alteration, or modification, executed by both parties. In the event that any provision of this License Agreement shall be held by a court or other tribunal of competent jurisdiction to be unenforceable, such provision will be enforced to the maximum extent permissible, and the remaining portions of this License Agreement shall remain in full force and effect. This License Agreement constitutes and contains the entire agreement between the parties with respect to the subject matter hereof and supersedes any prior oral or written agreements.

I hereby acknowledge that I have read and understand the foregoing License Agreement and agree that the action of installing the Program is an acknowledgment of my agreement to be bound by the terms and conditions of the License Agreement contained herein. I also acknowledge and agree that this License Agreement is the complete and exclusive statement of the agreement between Blizzard and me and that the License Agreement supersedes any prior or contemporaneous agreement, either oral or written, and any other communications between Blizzard and me.